HORSE RIDING
IN A
Weekend ™

HORSE RIDING
IN A
Weekend™

The easy way to learn to ride

Jane Holderness-Roddam

hamlyn

First published in Great Britain in 2004 by
Hamlyn, a division of Octopus Publishing Group Ltd
2–4 Heron Quays, London E14 4JP

Copyright © Octopus Publishing Group Ltd 2004

Distributed in the United States and Canada by
Sterling Publishing Co., Inc.
387 Park Avenue South, New York, NY 10016-8810

ISBN 0 600 60884 0

A CIP catalogue record for this book is available from
the British Library

Printed in China

10 9 8 7 6 5 4 3 2 1

contents

INTRODUCTION

'No hour of life is lost that is spent in the saddle.'

Winston Churchill

Riding is a wonderfully rewarding pastime that can be undertaken by young and old alike. There is so much on offer, to suit all ages and abilities – whether you want to aim for the top, enjoy the companionship and camaraderie between horse and rider, savour the outdoor life and all it has to offer, or just master the basics to enjoy the sport as a part-time amateur.

This book aims to set you on your way by providing straightforward explanations of what is involved, the basics required to take up riding and what you need to know to get started. While you can learn a huge amount in just a weekend, you will need several weeks to build up your confidence and improve your balance, co-ordination and ability before you can realistically expect to be a competent jockey.

Getting started

The book takes you on a step-by-step route, from planning how to get started and finding out more, to understanding the horse as an animal and how he thinks and reacts. You will discover how to communicate with him and get to know him; how to catch, lead and secure him safely; and how to tack him up. You will learn about the horse's basic needs to ensure his general health and well-being, and how to make sure you have the right horse to start you off. Throughout the book you will learn the correct terminology to use, and there is a section to help identify horses, from their colour and markings through to their general conformation.

There is also advice on how to book a lesson, how to dress for riding and what to expect when you arrive at the stables for your very first ride.

Days 1 and 2

How to tack up, get mounted, learn the basics of control and steering, and master the balance and co-ordination required to cope with the different paces – all these practical aspects are covered in detail on Days 1 and 2. Although you will not get as far as learning to jump on your first weekend, this is the next stage and is covered in the subsequent chapter. Throughout, handy tips and the secrets of success are provided to help you progress as quickly and easily as possible.

Moving on

Riding is one of those sports that brings together people of all backgrounds, ages and abilities, through their love of horses. It is a wonderful sport, which can be developed in numerous

Safety first
Safety tips are provided throughout the book. As a rider, you should be aware that horses can react unpredictably at times. They have the same feelings and basic instincts as we do and, however experienced they are, can be frightened or startled in unexpected situations. Always be aware and think ahead to avoid accidents.

different directions. The last section of the book explores some of the many opportunities available, from the simple joys of a trekking holiday to endurance riding, high-speed mounted games, competing in shows, and the classic sports of eventing, dressage and showjumping.

Through riding, the horse becomes a true friend and confidant, providing enjoyment, challenges and a complete way of life for those who want to enjoy these beautiful animals to the full. Once you have mastered the basics, the opportunities are endless.

Planning for progress
With sensible preparation and pre-planning, you can learn the first steps in this rewarding sport in just a couple of days, provided you take the trouble to study first exactly what is involved.

GETTING TO KNOW YOUR HORSE

Horses are man's best friends. To thousands of horse lovers there are no truer words, and the bond between horse and human has been recorded in infinite detail throughout history. It takes time, however, to build up a real partnership with a horse and it is important to understand the psychology of the horse to achieve this.

It should never be taken for granted how strong and potentially dangerous a horse can be if frightened, incorrectly handled or abused. Correctly and sensibly treated, however, the horse provides a unique friendship, something very special to care for, and has an outstanding ability to adapt to a myriad of different lifestyles.

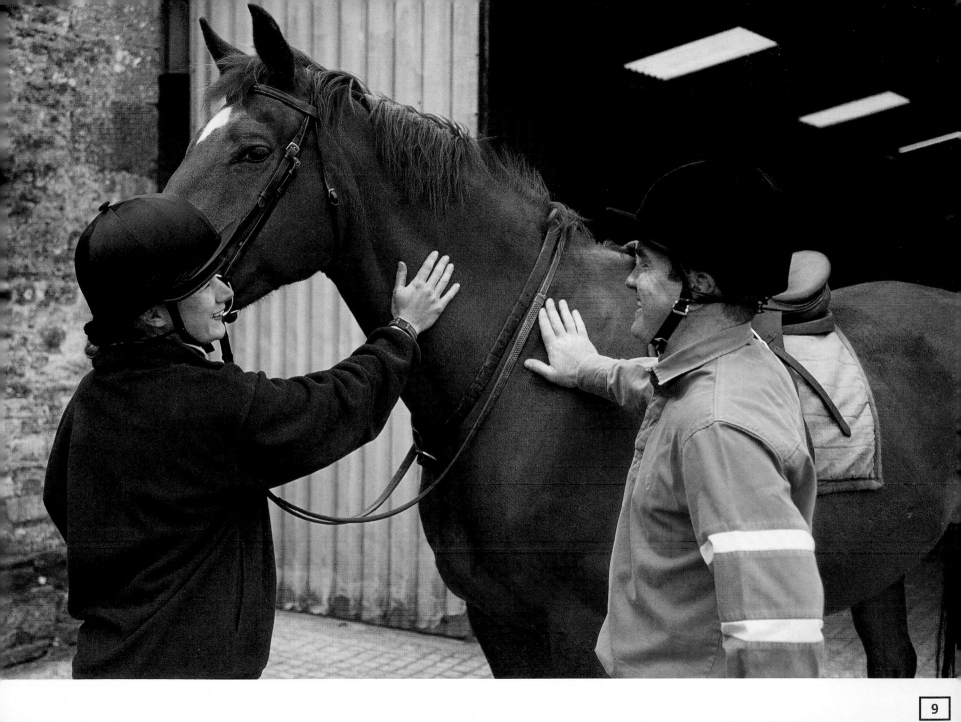

Making friends

Horses – and their smaller counterparts, ponies – are unique in that they have evolved over millions of years, eventually to become humankind's close friend over the centuries since their domestication some 4,000 years ago.

Throughout history, our ancestors have tamed and learned how to use the horse as a means of transport, work animal, warhorse and, more recently, a companion in leisure and sport. This wonderful animal has adapted magnificently to the challenges he has faced.

Today's horses and ponies are used in numerous different ways throughout the world and have adapted to domestication remarkably well. They appear to relish being ridden and driven, and are now recognized as being enormously useful in a variety of therapeutic situations.

The special bond between horse and human is easily seen as these two share a moment together.

History of horse behaviour

As the earth's surface has changed over the millennia, horses have roamed from continent to continent over vast land areas that were once joined together. Adapting to their surroundings and the hardships they endured, the 200 or so remaining different breeds gradually developed throughout the world from tiny, dog-sized creatures with three to five toes, into the more modern one-toed ancestor called *Equus* and, ultimately, into the horse we know today.

Being a prey animal, the horse's reactions and temperament have evolved from the instincts he needed to escape from danger in those early days. This is the reason why some more sensitive horses will react in panic by running away from danger, while others will buck their way out of a problem. It is also natural for horses to establish a kind of 'pecking order', with some being 'leaders' and others 'followers'.

First steps to friendship

Making friends with a horse requires some understanding of why horses behave as they do and what you need to look out for. Foremost in this is knowing how they communicate, as explained on pages 14–15. You can begin to understand what each horse likes and how he reacts by watching him with others. You will soon pick up his little ways and recognize his habits, character and how to get the best out of him.

As with children, patience is essential. Take your time and talk to your horse. The tone you use is the secret to success and quiet, soothing tones will encourage him to accept you and want to get to know you. Loud voices, quick and jerky movements, and a threatening posture will have the opposite effect.

Introducing yourself

- Stroking his neck is usually the best way to start to get to know your horse. Talk to him and stroke his nose and neck gently.

- Always approach from the front and be sure your horse is aware of your presence. Never frighten him by unexpected movement.

- Avoid feeding titbits on a regular basis. Your horse will come to expect these and may react with a kick or a bite if you fail to deliver.

- If you do offer a food treat to your horse, always keep your hand and fingers flat to avoid being chewed by mistake.

A special bond

Horses and ponies provide real friendships. They are wonderful companions – long-suffering, understanding and generous. Throughout history and in numerous storybooks and films, that special bond between human and horse never fails to enthral. Every week new stories appear of their incredible character, endurance or feats of brilliance, whether as a sport horse or in some other, less obvious, way.

Catching and leading

Getting your horse ready for your lesson is an opportunity to get to know each other and build your relationship, especially if you are able to catch the horse from the paddock, bring him into the yard or barn, and then tack him up. It also helps you to get used to the tack and how to put it on (see pages 42–45), which will become second nature after a couple of days.

Difficult to catch

Some horses are shy of being caught and start to walk away as you approach. It is best to stand still and offer the horse a 'treat' of a handful of feed until he comes up to you, which most will do if you don't make the mistake of rushing this important first stage. However, taking food into a field that has other horses in it should be a last resort, as they will tend to crowd around you.

Some horses are real characters and will try to avoid being caught, leading you a merry dance all around the place before finally relenting – if you are lucky!

Leading

Generally, horses are led from the left (near) side. If your horse walks freely forward, try to walk close to his shoulder. Some horses are rather idle and tend to hang back, making it a slow process to bring them to where you want them. Marching forward with a purposeful walk may help, or asking someone to help by clapping their hands at a safe distance behind the horse may do the trick.

The safety or quick-release knot ensures that you can undo the rope with one pull on the end. It is important to learn to tie a horse up correctly so ask your trainer to show you how to do this.

Tying up

Tie up the horse to an appropriate tie ring by using a safety 'quick-release' knot. In many stables, the horse's lead rope is tied to string (binder twine), as part of their safety policy. Should the horse pull back or become frightened for any reason, the string will break rather than the horse being hurt.

All horses not tied up in a stable should be watched carefully in case the unexpected happens. Gates and openings should be secured to ensure that a loose horse cannot stray on to roads or other dangerous areas.

✔ Shut the gate behind you when you enter the field.

✔ Approach the horse from the front and talk quietly to him as you do so.

✔ Stand still and let the horse come to you if he is a bit suspicious.

✔ Have the headcollar and rope ready to put on, but without making it too obvious.

Don't

✘ Run or chase after horses.

✘ Walk up behind a horse – always approach him from the front.

✘ Take food into the field if there are other horses there (unless absolutely necessary), as this will encourage crowding.

1

To catch your horse from the field, take a headcollar and lead rope. Call him by name – many respond to this, others do not – as you approach him slowly.

2

If he is happy to be caught, you can put the rope quietly around his neck. While holding him by the rope, bring the headcollar up over his nose.

3

Secure the headpiece over his head by fastening the buckle at the side. On occasion, reward him with some food.

Keep calm

Never chase a horse you are trying to catch or use quick or sudden movements – stand still and the horse will usually come to you, even if this takes a bit of time.

Communication

Understanding your horse is one of the most important aspects of being a good rider. So, how can you know what an animal that cannot speak is feeling, or understand what he is telling you?

The answer is simple – you look at his body language. Quite quickly, you will start to pick up signs that will help you to understand what he is thinking. The horse communicates most obviously by the expression in his eyes, while his ears indicate many different moods or emotions.

Learning to understand what your horse is 'saying' makes all the difference to the fun and enjoyment you experience. Some people miss out by not being interested in this aspect, but there is so much more to being with horses than just getting on and riding. Any relationship is a two-way thing and yours with the horse will really benefit from mutual understanding.

Take care

Some horses have their own ways of telling you something and will be much more expressive than others – quite soon, they may succeed in persuading you to give them a titbit or two! Be warned, however, that doing so can be dangerous, because when you or someone else does not respond in this way the horse may react like a spoilt child. He will not scream but he can certainly bite or kick, so do not get caught out. Be especially careful at a riding stables, where it is not so easy to bond with your horse owing to the number of other people who handle and ride him.

1
Making a face – this horse dislikes being peered at over his stable door and is saying 'Keep away from me.' You will need to approach with a quiet, encouraging word to change his mood from aggression to acceptance.

2
The dog has frightened this horse and is in danger of being kicked, which is understandable in such a situation.

Individual characters

As with humans, you need to understand the character of the individual horse in order to get the best from him. Ask yourself whether you believe him to be shy and timid, requiring a reassuring pat and quiet word before asking him to do something. Is he willing and immediately responsive, or is he one of those who is pretty fed up with his lot? The latter may need coaxing and cajoling into action with a firm and more demanding attitude on your part.

Horse watching
By watching how a particular horse behaves with others, you can learn a lot about how he responds to different situations.

3

This horse is a picture of contentment, with not a care in the world. He is lying down, relaxed and just watching what is going on in an interested way.

The right horse

Most riding stables take a lot of trouble to match the right horse to the right rider, but it helps if you understand how a horse thinks and reacts. As you get to know each other you will begin to build a relationship, which will develop as you progress through your lessons. Find out about his character from the stable staff: they know him best as they look after him every day. However, do not be put off if they are not particularly complimentary – he may still be a gem for a beginner!

4

'This looks pretty scary to me. I don't think I like my reflection!' A confidence-giving pat will help to persuade this horse that the water is not as dangerous as first appearances suggest.

Expressive ears

The most common ear positions can be interpreted as follows:

Ears flat back Anger, aggression: 'Get away from me!'

Ears back, with horse's hindquarters swung towards you Fear and aggression: 'I don't like you', 'I'm not sure about you' or 'Don't enter my space'.

Ears forward Contentment, interest: 'You have a friendly face', 'Let's make friends.'

Very forward Suspicion: 'Is it safe?', 'This might be frightening.'

One ear flicking forward and back Lack of confidence: 'I need support and encouragement.'

Learning about riding

For most people, riding is something you have seen or read about that has captured your imagination enough for you to want to find out more. This wonderful sport is unique in that two living beings learn to respond to each other and build up trust and respect, enabling a real partnership to develop.

There is nothing more exhilarating than feeling the wind on your face as you ride through the countryside, either with friends or alone – just you and the horse in harmony with each other. This is a very special experience, but does not come about without hard work, a few bruises, the odd scary moment or an occasional tumble!

Finding out more

Some mental preparation is also necessary to achieve success. If you have not already seen much riding at first hand, take the trouble to go to a riding stables and watch. Also talk to people who ride, so that you can begin to understand what is involved. Most riders are more than happy to tell you about their experiences.

You can also find out more about riding from books, videos and the Internet. It is worth learning a bit about the different types of riding to see what you might be interested in trying.

1

These three riders are cooling off after a rally at a Pony Club camp (see pages 96–97). Horses often want to lie down and roll in water. The rider on the right is raising her hands to keep her pony's head up and prevent him trying to get down. Always be alert to your horse's reactions in water, unless you want a ducking! Note that these riders are wearing safety helmets and body protectors, in case of falls or accidents.

2

These two prospective riders are visiting a riding school to find out what goes on by talking to two other riders at the end of their lesson. Most stables have an enclosed arena in which to work. This helps to keep novice riders within a confined area until they are competent enough to go out on a ride.

Safety first

Check that the stables has a health and safety policy, and whether or not you will be covered adequately by either your own insurance or that held by the riding school. Never be afraid to ask questions about these issues, so that you fully understand the implications should you have a fall or accident. Afterwards is too late!

Know your riding school

It is important to get to know the venue at which you intend to start riding and exactly what goes on there, as this helps you to be more confident and relaxed when you come to mounting and riding for the first time. Fear of the unknown is a common reaction, so it is a good plan to avoid this if possible. (See also pages 18–19.)

The stable yard should have a feeling of efficiency about it, with helpful staff who look after you, their client. The general neatness and tidiness will often be an indication of its standards. Most countries have an approval scheme for riding schools run through their national equestrian body, so check that your chosen stables has an approval certificate. The atmosphere at a riding stables can tell you a lot about how well it is run, so check whether the horses and staff seem happy and willing to do what is expected of them.

Booking a lesson

Once you have decided that you really want to take up riding, you will need to identify a suitable stables at which to learn. You may already know of somewhere through friends, or have been recommended a particular riding school by a professional such as a vet or farrier. Local saddlery stores can also give useful advice.

Preparation and planning

You can, of course, simply book a lesson over the telephone, but it is always best to visit and meet the staff. They will go through the procedures with you and give guidance on suitable clothing to wear. Most schools have a selection of safety helmets for hire and it is worth finding out from them first hand what is recommended.

Book a lesson at a time that suits both you and the school, making sure you are able to allow yourself enough time to get there and organize yourself to be ready for your allotted time. Most schools are booked up well in advance, so if you are late it is unlikely that you will get your full time and as much attention as you would if you were ready and waiting.

1

This learner-rider finds out from the instructor exactly what is involved and books a lesson.

Riding hats

Make sure the hat you wear:

• Is the right size for you.
• Is up to the latest approved riding standards.
• Has a safe and secure fastening.
• Is in good condition, with the outer shell intact.

The chin strap must always be fastened when you are on the horse.

2
A neat and tidy yard with contented-looking horses in traditional, English-style stables.

Make sure that the school appears well run overall and bear the following questions in mind.

✔ Is the muck heap kept neat and tidy? This will often indicate how well the rest of the yard is run.

✔ Is there a safe area or school (arena) in which beginners can learn?

✔ Did you receive a friendly welcome?

✔ Does the school have a health and safety policy (see pages 16–17)?

✔ Is the school approved by a recognized riding organization (see pages 16–17)?

✔ Are the horses suitable for beginners?

First-lesson gear

The instructor will probably recommend that, for a first lesson, you wear a pair of strong trousers or jeans, and lace-up shoes or boots with a heel and a smooth sole. Gloves are also a good idea, and the school should provide a safety helmet with a chin-strap fastening. (See also pages 20–21.)

Your first horse

A good first horse will be an experienced 'schoolmaster' who has already taught many people to ride. He will be quiet, steady and tolerant, and seem to understand the importance of taking his rider very slowly during the first few important lessons.

Basic equipment

When taking up riding, the most important thing to think about is safety – so make sure that what you wear is safe for the job, practical and, of course, comfortable. Some people put themselves through agony by failing to appreciate how much friction there may be on their legs when riding, so it is most important to ensure you have thick trousers or jodhpurs, or use some undergear to prevent blisters and rubs until your skin becomes hardened. Gloves are also important as they protect your hands. Different types of riding may merit different kit, but the essentials to get started are listed here.

Basic kit

- Up-to-date, recommended hat with a secure fastening. Before buying, check that the hat is an approved design and conforms to the safety standards of the country. Hats should be of the right size and fit snugly, and must be secured at all times when mounted.
- Short boots with a low heel, or long leather or rubber riding boots are ideal. They must fit closely to your leg and have a relatively smooth sole so that they do not stick in the stirrups. Calf-length half-chaps used with short jodhpur boots are also popular.
- Jodhpurs are specifically designed for riders and have knee padding positioned to prevent friction rubs. Breeches (a shorter-legged version) are good for use with long boots or half-chaps. Tough jeans or trousers can be used if you are just starting at walk, but are not recommended for serious riding.
- Gloves made from string or fabric – especially those with a rubber pimple insert on the palm – give good grip and will protect hands from blisters or sores caused by rubs from the reins.
- A body protector is a wise investment, especially when you progress to serious riding and jumping. Buy one that is comfortable to wear but also protective. Choose one that is recommended by your riding school and of an approved safety design. Many schools supply these for use on loan.

Buying riding gear

For more formal wear, it is possible to find nearly everything you will need in your local tack shop. If you want to take part in a specific type of competition, it is always worth checking what gear you need before investing in any special kit.

When buying riding clothes, remember that you need a bit of room to move, especially with jackets, to allow you freedom to mount and dismount. Tight clothing of whatever kind is not recommended for any type of riding. If you live in a cold climate it is worth getting boots large enough to take some really thick socks: icy toes are no fun at all on an early-morning ride!

There is nothing more frustrating than suffering from sores or blisters so do take care to ensure you are wearing adequate clothing, especially on the most vulnerable areas – the legs, knees, ankles and hands.

1

For everyday riding it is not necessary to be too formal and this rider is kitted out appropriately, with a safety skullcap, riding jeans, half-chaps, boots and gloves. She is also carrying a stick, which may not be necessary for a beginner.

2

This is the more formal kit used for general competition. It includes a dark jacket, white hunting-tie, long boots, breeches and gloves. Note the rider's hair neatly secured in a hairnet beneath the skull hat and dark cover.

The horse's basic needs

The horse's needs are very similar to our own, in that he requires adequate food, water, shelter and exercise in order to remain healthy. In their natural state, horses roam in herds on the plains, and most domestic horses would still prefer to live outside, where they can pick and choose which vegetation to eat and are able to wander around at will.

The grass-kept horse

Some horses and ponies are better suited to living outdoors than others and they will grow warm, thick winter coats. The build-up of grease in the coat of field-kept horses provides adequate warmth for most horses. Some other breeds, however, such as Arabs and Thoroughbreds, will require extra help in the form of food concentrates and rugs in order to keep warm outside, or will need to be stabled.

To keep a horse outdoors, you will need:

- A well-fenced field with a safe, secure gate, padlocked or alarmed if necessary.
- Adequate grass for the horse's needs: 0.4–0.8 hectares (1–2 acres) is the minimum area for a pony (more for a horse), but this will depend on the quality of the grass.
- Companions, if sufficient land is available. Horses cope well on their own, but are basically herd animals and enjoy the company of others.
- Fresh water freely available, from either a clean, free-flowing stream or a water trough.
- Shelter from the elements, from either trees and hedges or a field shelter. Outdoor rugs may be necessary for certain weather conditions.

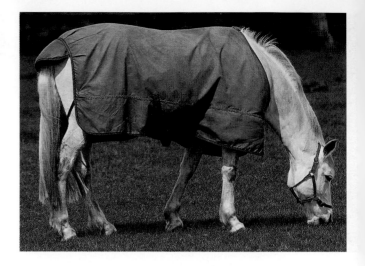

1

Weatherproof rugs, usually known as New Zealand rugs, must fit correctly and the leg straps must be crossed through each other to give protection to sensitive skin from chafing or rubs.

Pasture management
- Keep the field free of poisonous plants (check these with your national agriculture authority) and any items likely to cause injury.
- Skip out the field regularly to keep it free of droppings.
- Rest the field periodically to allow the grass to regrow.
- Worm horses regularly (see pages 24–25).

The stabled horse

The stabled horse requires a great deal of time and commitment to ensure that he is well looked after. Being confined for too long without exercise is unnatural, so he must be exercised daily and, if possible, turned out in a paddock or at least led out to eat grass. Confinement also makes it difficult for the horse to keep warm, so he will need appropriate rugs in cold weather or at night.

Water, hay or haylage should be freely available, unless the horse is on a restricted diet. Bedding should be absorbent and protect the horse from injuring himself when lying down. Suitable types include straw, paper shreddings, shavings, peat and rubber matting, all of which must be kept clean.

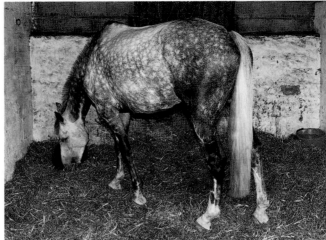

2

These two horses are happily wandering across a well-sheltered paddock. If possible, avoid keeping a horse on his own – being herd animals, horses enjoy the companionship of their own kind.

3

This stabled horse is tucking into his evening feed. Note the full hay rack and bucket of water in the corner. Straw bedding is used here and is warm, absorbent and comfortable.

Suggested routine for a stabled horse

07.00 Feed, water and hay. Change rugs if necessary. Muck out stable.
10.00 Ridden exercise, or turn out until evening feed time.
12.00 Skip out stable and replenish hay and water.
14.00 Exercise (if not turned out).
16.00 Groom, replace rugs if necessary, skip out stable.
17.00 Feed, water and hay.
20.00 Final check, top up hay and water.

Rugs

There is a huge variety of different rugs available. These range from light summer sheets and fly sheets to really warm duvet-type stable rugs and weatherproof outdoor rugs designed to cope with the wettest days. Whatever its purpose, it is important to check that the rug fits comfortably and is the right size for the horse.

The healthy horse

The horse is entitled to the best possible care, regardless of whether he lives out in a paddock, is stabled, or enjoys a combination of both. Throughout this book, we encourage you to get to know about every aspect of this special animal on which you intend to learn to ride. It is only by really understanding all about your horse that you will get the very best out of him in the long term.

Exercise

If the horse lives in a paddock, exercise is easy because he roams around freely while grazing, as he would in his natural state. The stabled horse, however, needs to be ridden or exercised daily to maintain health and fitness (see pages 22–23). A horse-walker or exerciser allows several horses to be exercised at one time, moving in a controlled way. These mechanized devices allow horses to be walked safely in a circle, in separate compartments, at roughly five miles an hour.

Shoeing

Regular shoeing or trimming of the hooves, usually about every six weeks, is essential to the horse's well-being. Some horses will require more frequent care, depending on the hardness of their feet, the terrain over which they are travelling, and the wear and tear to feet or shoes due to their level of work.

A qualified farrier is a regular visitor to most stables. He has been trained to care for the horse's hooves and to keep them well balanced through correct trimming and shoeing. Shoes are used to protect the hooves of hard-working horses from too much wear.

Beware lameness

Metal shoes are nailed to the hoof wall, and if this is not carried out correctly the horse may go lame. Hoof lameness is one of the most common reasons for preventing horses and ponies being ridden.

Worming

Horses need to be wormed regularly. Depending on the drug used, worming is generally carried out at 6- to 12-week intervals. The vet will advise on the best types and dosages to use, as different brands are designed to be effective at particular times of the year to destroy the different worm larvae. If your horse is losing weight, has a dull coat and appears not to be thriving, worms could well be the problem.

Teeth care

The horse's teeth require rasping at least once a year by a specialist equine dentist or vet. Teeth tend to wear unevenly, making it difficult for the horse to eat, as well as causing sores in the mouth resulting in head tossing.

Signs of health
- Bright eyes.
- Glossy coat.
- Normal temperature.
- Normal pulse.
- Normal breathing.
- Adequately conditioned for type of horse and exercise being given.
- General sense of well-being.

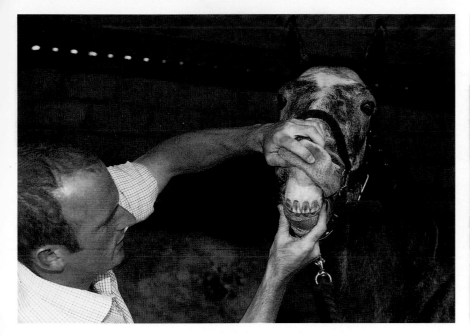

1

The vet is inspecting this horse's mouth for any signs of injury or soreness before rasping the teeth. He will usually place a special gag on the horse to prevent injury.

2

Worming doses can be given as a paste inserted via an applicator into the horse's mouth. They can also be given as pellets mixed into the horse's feed. However, many horses waste the pellets as they become wise to the less palatable ingredients.

Vaccinations

Different countries require or recommend certain vaccinations or preventative care, such as anti-tetanus or 'flu injections. Most of these require a basic course, which might involve up to three primary injections, before an annual or biannual booster. All injections should be recorded in the horse's passport or vaccination record. Take care not to allow the renewal date to overrun, as most records become invalid if injections are not given within a specified time.

Keep up to date
Prevention is always better than cure, so keep a record of vaccination dates, worming, teeth care and shoeing.

Grooming

Grooming is one of the most rewarding jobs in looking after horses. Even if you ride at a riding school where your horse has already been groomed for you, it is well worth taking the time to find out what is involved. It is a great way to bond with your favourite mount, and gives you the opportunity to get to know him and become involved with his daily needs.

The grass-kept horse needs to be tidied up daily but not groomed too thoroughly, as the grease in his coat keeps him warm. Even in hot climates, there may be a considerable drop in temperature at night and most horses much prefer living out without a rug, except in very cold weather (see pages 22–23). For stabled horses, however, grooming is an important part of their day and one that most of them thoroughly enjoy.

1

Grooming starts with a thorough brush over the whole neck and body, progressing from the front of the horse to the rear on both sides. Always brush following the lie of the coat. Depending on the degree of mud or dirt and the sensitivity of the horse's skin, you can start with a dandy brush, or rubber curry comb or glove, and then use the body brush. Be sensitive to whether your horse is ticklish and don't be too forceful if he is.

2

Once you have finished the body, take a little time to brush the head gently (being careful not to knock the face bones) and behind and around the ears. Some horses are quite sensitive here and hand-rubbing these areas may be the answer. Sponge the eyes and nostrils to remove any dirt or mucus, then the lips. Check that there are no sores in the creases of the lips caused by rubs from the bit or noseband. Using a separate sponge, gently lift the tail and wipe off any dung or dirt around the dock area under the tail.

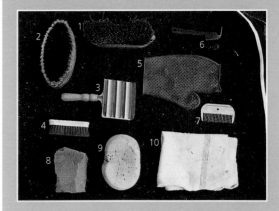

Basic grooming kit

3

Next, pick out the horse's feet using a hoofpick. Run your hand down the horse's leg and pick up his foot. Hold it at a height that is easy for both you and the horse. Be aware that the horse could flick his foot up – keep your head away from danger of this happening.

4

To remove mud, dirt and stones, work the point of the hoofpick with a downward pull, from the top of the cleft on either side of the frog towards the point of the frog (see pages 32–33). Always check that the shoes are safe and secure, with no loose nails. Apply hoof oil or grease to the hooves two to three times a week to help keep these in good condition. You can also oil his hooves if you are going to a competition or someone is coming to see the horse, to help him look especially smart.

1 Dandy brush For removing mud, sweat and loose hairs from unclipped horses.
2 Body brush For grooming summer coats and clipped horses.
3 Curry comb For cleaning the body brush.
4 Water brush For dampening and laying the hair of the forelock, mane and tail.
5 Rubber glove For hand-rubbing sensitive areas to remove mud, sweat and loose hairs.
6 Hoofpick For picking out mud and debris from horse's hooves.
7 Comb For tidying and pulling manes and tails.
8 Face sponge For refreshing around the eyes and nostrils.
9 Dock sponge For cleaning up around the dock (tailbone) area.
10 Stable rubber For a final polish.

The right horse for you

To really enjoy riding at its best, you must first experience the thrill of it all with the right horse. To achieve this, a number of factors should be taken into account.

Size

This is probably the most important factor for a beginner. If the horse is too big, he can appear somewhat intimidating; too small, and you start to feel that you should not be up there anyway!

Most horses, small or large, are very capable of carrying an average-sized adult. However, you will feel more comfortable on one that is the right size for you. The conformation of the horse and his shape also plays an important part, as some small horses can be incredibly strong, while others can be light-framed and incapable of carrying anyone too heavy.

It is important to remember that it is not just the size or weight of the rider that is important – the saddle and other equipment can significantly increase the load.

Temperament

A suitable temperament is vital and most riding schools only take on horses or ponies that have proved themselves suitable for beginners. They must be steady and reliable, not too quick, yet responsive enough to react when indicated to do so by an inexperienced rider. All in all, these animals are required to be the perfect mount for a less-than-perfect rider!

Pony size
A pony is generally accepted as being less than 162 cm (15 hands) in height, and a horse as 162 cm (15 hands) or over.

Choice of mount
Your riding school will decide which horse is most suitable for you as a beginner. Staff will take into account your size, age, weight and height when making this choice.

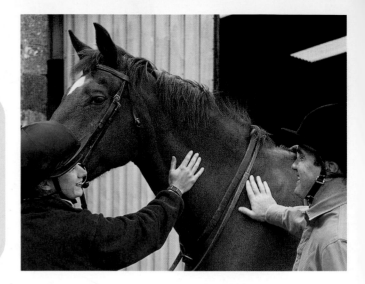

1

The beginner needs a calm steady horse who will not react too quickly and will be forgiving to confused commands from inexperienced riders.

Age

Various breeds of horse and pony, and their cross-breds, are suited to the role of beginner's mount, but good training over a period of time usually means that a slightly older animal is a better bet.

It is not usually a good idea to put a complete beginner on a horse younger than six-years-old, as the horse is unlikely to have had sufficient experience. A horse is usually broken-in for riding when he is three to four years old, and is not considered fully mature until he reaches the age of six. The young horse then needs a gradual build-up of work in order to become physically strong enough to cope with the demands placed on him.

Different breeds

2
These two riders look happy and confident on the two differently sized horses, each of which are manageable for their respective riders.

3
The small rider is now on the larger horse who is far too big and strong for her, whilst the larger rider is too big and heavy on the light-framed horse.

'Hot-blooded' breeds
The Arab – the oldest pure breed – and the Thoroughbred are the only two 'hot-blooded' breeds in the world, being the most finely bred and fastest breeds. Although other breeds do race, it is these two who are most associated with racing.

Ponies
Children generally start on ponies because of their size. Ponies are great favourites and have a rather more independent nature than their larger friend, the horse. They tend to be stronger and tougher for their size, and full of character. They can be as generous as you could want or extremely stubborn, getting their own way far too often. This trait can, however, be very useful when you need to point out such behaviour to a child who is being equally difficult!

Preparation and meeting your instructor

It is well worth getting to know your trainer or instructor when you first visit the riding school. While they will often be busy with other clients, they should also be able to meet you and explain what goes on, so that you are familiar with the routine. You may also have the opportunity to meet other learners who can share their experiences with you (see pages 16–19).

Familiarize yourself

Watch carefully what goes on, so that you get to know whether your horse will be in his stable or in the yard and how will you find him; whether you will be involved in grooming and tacking him up; where you will be expected to mount the horse and how this works; and where each part of the lesson takes place.

If you are borrowing a hat and/or back protector, familiarize yourself with where these are kept. Find out who you should talk to about ensuring you have the right size and that the fastenings are adjusted correctly.

Establishing a good rapport with your instructor will add to your enjoyment of the lesson and help to increase your confidence as a rider.

Your instructor

You should always check that your instructor is qualified to teach – not all of them are. At the very least, they should be experienced and recommended by others before you allow yourself to be taught. Most good schools have approval, registration or membership of the relevant training departments of the national equestrian society. Do not be fobbed off with a young trainee, who will not have sufficient knowledge or experience to ensure you are given that all-important good start.

A good instructor, in whom you have complete faith, makes all the difference. Once you have started, it is important to try to stay with the same one so that you build up a good relationship and progress logically. Remember to ask your instructor any obvious questions before you start your lesson – you will certainly have masses to ask afterwards!

Positive attitude

Remember the most important aspect of trying anything new is to be positive in your attitude and confident that you can achieve your aims. Listen carefully to the instructions and don't be afraid to ask about anything you are not sure of.

Preparation pays dividends

You will find your lesson even more rewarding if you have thoroughly prepared yourself, and discovered how to find your way around both the horse (as explained throughout this chapter) and the tack he is wearing (see pages 42–47).

Are you fit to ride?

Check that you have covered the following areas:

✔ Exercises and stretches.

✔ Walking.

✔ Running or cycling.

✔ Good diet.

(See also pages 38–39.)

Do you have?

Make sure you have equipped yourself with:

✔ Hat.

✔ Gloves.

✔ Sensible boots.

✔ Jodhpurs or tough trousers.

(See also pages 20–21.)

Points of the horse

'Points of the horse' is the phrase used to describe the terms that identify the various different parts of the horse. It is worth knowing as many of these as possible, so that you can understand which part of the horse is being talked about when you tack him up or ride him.

Understanding terms

Some terms cover a fairly large area of the horse's body. These include the 'hindquarters' (or just 'quarters'), which is a general term for the rear end of the horse, and the 'forehand', which is the front end. The left side of the horse is termed the 'near side', and is generally the side people work from, while the right is known as the 'off side'. Some countries use local terms to describe certain areas of the horse's body, but you will quickly pick these up as you progress.

Some terms can be quite confusing to start with. For example: 'forelock', which is the part of the horse's mane that comes from between his ears down his face, could easily be confused with 'fetlock', which is the lowest joint in the leg before the pastern joins the hoof (see opposite). These are often used as trick questions when you have an equestrian quiz!

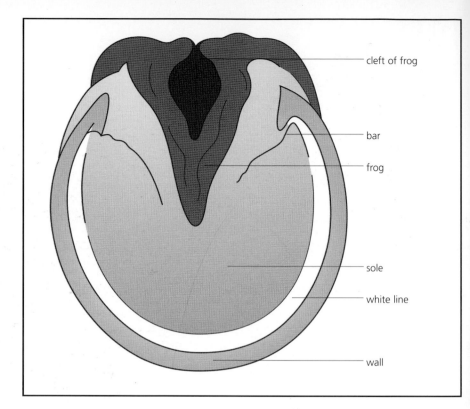

- cleft of frog
- bar
- frog
- sole
- white line
- wall

Measuring horses

A horse's height is measured in hands (1 hand = 4 inches) or centimetres from the top of the withers to the ground. Bone – an indication of strength – is measured just below the knee around the cannon bone.

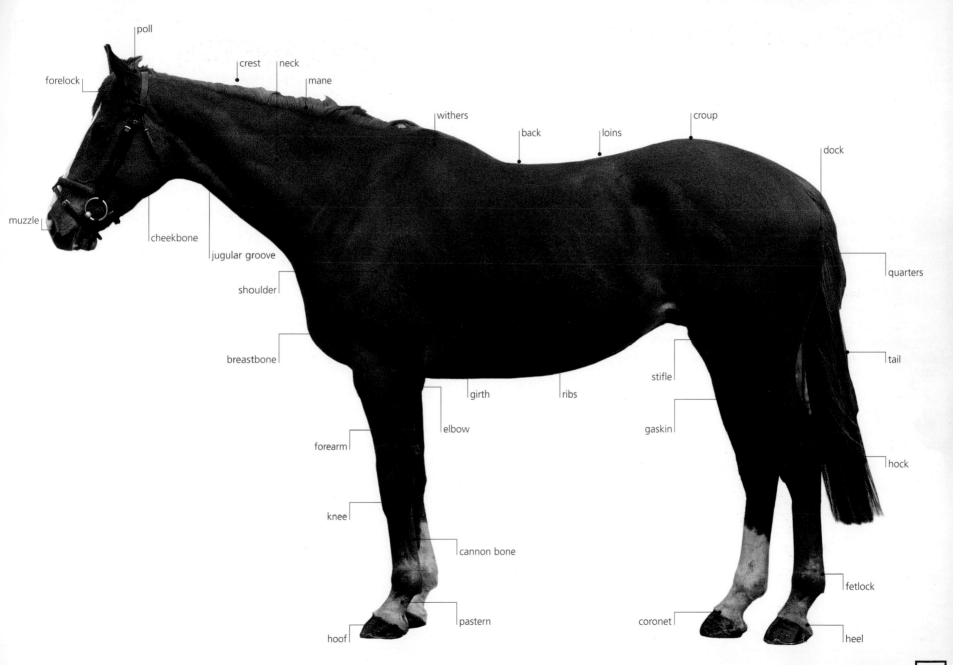

poll

crest   neck

forelock   mane

withers

croup

muzzle   back   loins   dock

cheekbone

jugular groove   quarters

shoulder

breastbone   tail

stifle

girth   ribs

gaskin

elbow

forearm   hock

knee

cannon bone

fetlock

coronet

pastern

hoof   heel

points of the horse   **33**

Colours

Horses come in a bewildering array of colours, depending on their breed or type. Some of these are solid colours, others have distinctive body markings. Head and leg markings also vary enormously, although they usually fall into a few basic categories.

Appaloosa A versatile American breed, distinctive for its unique colouring that is divided into eight different patterns.

Dappled grey Most greys become lighter as they age, usually ending up almost white. However, there are several colours, ranging from the dark 'iron grey' to a 'flea-bitten grey' which has small tufts of brown or black hair scattered over the body.

Dark brown A smart, distinctive colour with a lighter brown around the muzzle.

Palomino A beautiful golden colour with a white mane and tail.

Breed colours

Certain colours or markings can indicate the age of a breed. The dun, a golden to golden-brown colour with a black mane and tail, is one of these and several ancient breeds have this as a strong basic colour, such as the Norwegian Fjord. Others have distinctive colour characteristics, including the Exmoor pony, with 'mealy' eyes and muzzle; the Appaloosa, with striking spots and white membrane around the rims of the eyes; and the Norwegian Fjord, with a distinctive black centre line along the white mane.

Pinto A distinctively marked horse with white and any other colour markings. In Britain, the pinto is called a piebald (black and white) or skewbald (any other colour and white).

Dun An ancient colour, consisting of a gold body with a black mane and tail and black points.

Bay A nut-brown colour with black points. This one has a white face and stockings, with excessive hair on the legs known as 'feathers'.

Paint These youngsters are having a great time and are showing a variety of white markings. They are usually referred to as 'paint' horses in the USA and 'coloured' horses elsewhere.

Markings

Face markings

These are described according to their shape on the horse's head (see below). Flesh marks are pink-skinned areas lacking pigment, usually found on the muzzle around the nostrils. These areas are often prone to sunburn.

Blaze with a flesh mark extending over the nostrils.

Star and stripe with flesh mark on the nose.

Star with tiny snip on the bottom of the muzzle.

Other markings

Ermine marks Black spots or white hairs around the pastern or coronet band.

Zebra markings Black stripes on the back of the forearm or front of the second thigh, usually found on duns.

Black points Black legs, found on duns, bays (see below) or browns.

Leg markings

These are named according to the amount of white on the leg and often include the name of the area represented. A full white area generally corresponds with a white hoof on that leg.

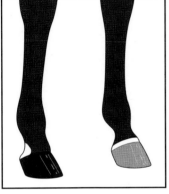 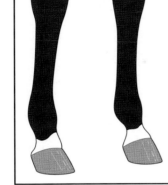 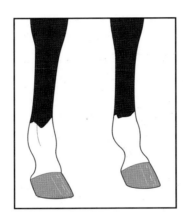 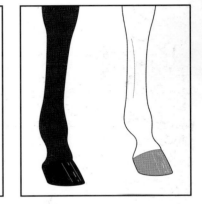

Heel or coronet Denotes a very little white in that area.

Pastern White below the fetlock joint.

Sock Includes white over the fetlock joint, up to halfway up the leg.

Stocking White reaches up to the knee or hock joint, but does not include the joints.

White leg Extends above the knee or hock joint.

Pre-riding exercises

Most of us get stiff following exercise to which we are unaccustomed. Riding is no exception, but with a little extra effort your muscles and body will quickly adapt.

A physical sport

Despite the fact that you sit on top of the horse, riding is incredibly physical. Your body moves with every step the horse takes, and you need to adapt and co-ordinate your balance to move in unison with the motion.

Some horses are quite broad, others narrow, and your body will have to get used to the movement as you sit astride. It is not difficult, but some people can take a little time to adapt.

Stretching exercises

Doing some simple stretching exercises will increase your suppleness and tone your muscles. Taking the time to do a quick warm up before you go riding will help to prevent aching muscles afterwards and enable you to get even more enjoyment from riding.

Ask your riding or fitness trainer for a few exercises to practise, or use the leg stretches shown opposite. Everyone is a little different and you will find some things easy and others more difficult, depending on your shape and build and your general level of fitness.

Fitness exercise

Any fitness exercise will help – try some of the following:

- Walking and running.
- Games such as tennis and football.
- Swimming.
- Aerobic exercises, such as sit-ups and step-ups.
- Skipping.
- Bending and stretching exercises.

Cycling

Cycling is a particularly good fitness exercise for riders, as it gets your leg muscles into shape. Practise allowing your heel to drop down on the pedal, in a similar way to how you will have to ride. Riding up off the seat will also help to strengthen your back and leg muscles, and will improve the balance and co-ordination that are so essential for riding.

Caution
If you have any physical problems, talk to your trainer or doctor to make sure that riding will not aggravate the condition. Sometimes a different type of saddle can be used to give greater comfort.

Diet

Your diet is also very important, especially as you become a more proficient rider.

- As riding is such a physical sport, be sure to keep yourself well hydrated with plenty of drinks, especially in hot weather, both before and after your lesson or ride.

- A high-energy diet will ensure you have enough calories on board to cope with your lesson and prevent you feeling tired afterwards.

1

Inner thigh stretch This stretch will help your muscles to adapt to sitting astride the horse. With feet facing forwards and legs wide apart, shift your weight on to your right leg, until you feel the stretch on the inner thigh of your left leg. Hold for ten seconds, then repeat with the other leg.

2

Quad stretch This will stretch the quadriceps muscles in your thighs and exercise your knee. Stand with your feet together, then use your left hand to pick up your left leg as shown. Hold for ten seconds, then repeat with the other leg.

3

Calf stretch This exercise will help to stretch your calf muscles, and generally utilize all your leg muscles. Position yourself as shown, with your weight on your right leg, and feel the stretch in the back of your left leg. Hold for 20 seconds, then repeat with the other leg.

DAY 1: THE FIRST STEPS

After all the preparation and the knowledge you have gained, you are now ready to put it all into practice!

Tacking up and mastering the act of mounting are the first hurdles to be tackled. Some find it all very easy, while others require a little more practice. As with anything, once you have mastered the technique, it is simply a matter of practice and accustoming untrained muscles to cope with new demands.

Putting on the saddle

Although many riding schools will have the horse tacked up ready for you to save time, you still need to know how to do this yourself so that you can be sure it has been correctly put on, but also so that you will be able to do it yourself, if necessary.

It is important to know how and where the saddle fits so that you will be able to identify any discomfort or soreness caused to the horse if, for example, the saddle presses down on the wither. Ask your trainer to explain how the saddle should fit and what to look out for.

Learning goal

Practise putting on the saddle, following the method described. Be sure to avoid banging the horse's back or side as you put the saddle on to his back and slide it into position.

1

Place the numnah or saddle pad over the horse's back near the wither and slide it into position along the lie of the coat. Check that it is not wrinkled on the off side: if this goes unnoticed, it can cause a pressure rub.

2

Take the saddle with the girth attached on the off side and place it on top of the numnah or pad, easing it gently back into position.

3

Pull the numnah up into the front arch of the saddle, to prevent pressure on the wither when the girth is tightened.

Preparation

Collect your tack from the tack room. Check that you have everything you need:

• Saddle with stirrup irons and leathers in place.
• Numnah or saddle pad
• Girth of the correct length for the horse.
• Bridle (see pages 44–45).

Now check that all the tack is clean and in good condition. When you are satisfied that everything is in order, take all your tack to the stable (or wherever your horse is) and tie him up to prevent him wandering about.

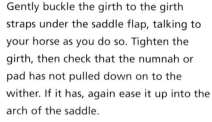

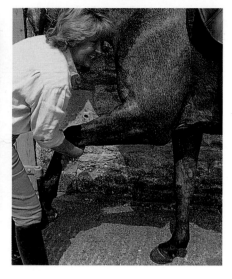

Removing the saddle

To take off the saddle, lift the saddle flap on the near side and undo the girth, making sure it does not drop and hit the horse's leg. Lift the saddle up off the horse's back before sliding it off sideways towards you. Pick up the girth and lay it across the saddle as you slide it off the horse.

4

Lift the girth and quietly drop the unattached end over the saddle, so that it hangs down on the off side – with nervous horses, walk around to the off side and lift the girth down. Bend down and bring the girth through under the horse's belly.

5

Gently buckle the girth to the girth straps under the saddle flap, talking to your horse as you do so. Tighten the girth, then check that the numnah or pad has not pulled down on to the wither. If it has, again ease it up into the arch of the saddle.

6

Gently lift the horse's near foreleg and stretch it forward, to ensure that no folds of skin are caught between the elbow and girth. Repeat on the off side. Finally, check that everything is in the correct place.

Saddle position

The saddle should not be placed so far forward that it interferes with the movement of the horse's shoulder. Run your hand down under the front of the saddle to ensure that it is behind the movable shoulder blade and will not impede its action.

Make sure you understand the dangers of a saddle with too wide a tree, which will sit too low on the horse's back, or too narrow a tree, which will have the opposite effect.

Putting on the bridle

Once you have put on the saddle, make sure you have everything to hand for your ride, including hat, gloves and stick (if necessary).

Preparation

If a martingale is used it should be put on before the saddle, as one end is attached between the horse's front legs to the girth. The other end of a standing martingale is attached to a cavesson noseband (see page 107), while the ends of a running martingale slide over the reins. Rein stops must be used with a running martingale to prevent the rings catching on the billets or buckles of the reins that are attached to the bit.

Before putting on the bridle, undo the throatlatch and noseband, release the headcollar buckle and put it round the horse's neck.

Learning goal

Practise putting the bridle on and doing up the throatlatch and noseband in the correct sequence.

1
Put the reins over the horse's head and slide them down his neck. Hold the bridle with your right hand and with your left hand ease the bit into the horse's mouth, by putting your thumb into his mouth at the side where there are no teeth. Most horses will open up quickly, some take a bit more persuading.

2
Lift the bridle up and ease the headpiece gently over one ear, then the other. Straighten the bridle if necessary, and pull out the forelock so that it hangs over the top of the browband.

Using a neckstrap

A neckstrap can be used for security. This consists of a strap (an old stirrup leather is ideal) placed around the horse's neck for the rider to hold on to if necessary.

3

Take hold of the throatlatch and fasten it. You should be able to fit your hand sideways between the horse's cheek and the throatlatch. Any tighter than this could restrict his breathing when he draws in his head.

4

The next stage involves fastening the noseband. This horse has a cross-over (grakle or figure-of-eight) noseband, which helps to prevent opening of the mouth (see pages 106–107). It has four separate straps that join together: the top two fasten above the bit, the lower two beneath the bit. Check that the cross-over is central on the front of the horse's nose (this area should have a soft pad for comfort).

5

Check over the bridle and make sure all keepers are in place, so that there are no straps flapping around.

Western tack

Western riding is extremely popular, particularly in America where it originated from Spanish influences. The very comfortable saddle was originally designed for horses and riders who would spend hours, or even days, out on the prairies. Western riding today varies from gentle trail rides to serious competitive classes (see pages 116–117 and 142–143).

Learning goal
Practise the technique of neck reining by applying gentle pressure against the neck to turn the horse in either direction with the reins.

Saddle
The flat base of the saddle spreads the weight across the horse's back, while the deep seat keeps the rider secure. Many Western saddles are beautifully decorated.

Fenders These wide, long leather straps support the stirrups, protecting the rider's legs.
Horn Most Western saddles have a high pommel or 'horn' at the front for tying on the lasso – a rope used to catch steers on the prairies.
Cinch This is the Western girth and is secured by means of a thick leather thong wrapped around a ring and tightened as necessary.

Bridle
Often ornately decorated, the Western bridle is simple in design and straightforward to put on, as it does not have any type of noseband.

Slit-eared headpiece Some designs have a slit-eared headpiece, rather than the browband shown in the photographs here. The headpiece is specially shaped and split to allow one or both of the horse's ears through to hold it in place. There is no throatlatch with these bridles.
Reins These consist of two long, separate straps coming from a long, generally curved, curb bit. Western riders ride one-handed and apply gentle pressure to the horse's neck from the rein to change direction ('neck reining'). Some designs are similar to English closed reins but have a single length of leather called a quint or romal attached at the end to act as a whip.

In case you fall
Remember that the stetson is not protective in the case of a fall. However, falls from a Western saddle are relatively rare because of the security offered by the deep seat.

1

The saddle has been placed on the horse. Note the double-folded saddle blanket used under the saddle – traditionally, this acted as bedding for the rider at night. The leather thong is being tightened between the ring on the saddle and the cinch, in order to girth up the horse.

✔ Ensure you keep your weight central.

✔ Use a suitable bit designed for a light touch appropriate for the horse.

✔ Remember Western-trained horses respond to the lightest touch.

Don't

✗ Expect a Western horse to move in the same way as a conventionally trained horse.

✗ Forget Western saddles are designed to be ridden with a long leg position.

2

Western bridles do not have a noseband and the slit-eared designs do not have a throatlatch, so putting them on the horse is very straightforward.

3

Trail riding takes you over all types of terrain. Your horse must therefore be well trained and sure-footed, happy to go through water or up and down steep tracks.

Rider gear

Western riders generally wear jeans, with or without chaps (protective leather leggings), with decorative but strong elegant leather boots. They also wear decorative, fringed shirts. The stetson – a wide-brimmed hat designed to protect against the sun – completes the kit.

Pre-mount checklist

You now understand the basic requirements necessary to start riding and should be ready to get going. You have prepared yourself mentally and physically, have the right gear (or at least enough to start), and you know your way around the stables and the horse himself. You have met your instructor and know about the type of things you will be asked to do. The day of your first lesson has finally arrived.

Learning goal
Think of all you have been taught and remember the following: safety first, preparation, motivation and achievement.

Before your lesson
Work through the following checklist:

- Make sure you have had a drink and something to eat before you set off for the stables.
- Check that you have your hat, suitable footwear and gloves with you before you leave.
- Do not be late – riding schools are busy places.
- Be sure to introduce yourself, so that the staff know you have arrived.
- Enjoy the experience!

1

Learning to lead your horse confidently is important. Try to keep near his shoulder with him walking forward well so you are aware of where and what he is doing.

Your instructor
Your instructor will need to work through his or her own checklist:

- Ensure the horse is suitable for you and the tack is correctly adjusted, in particular that the stirrup irons are a suitable size.
- Check that the horse is ready for the lesson.
- Explain to you how the lesson will be conducted.
- Check that the girth is tight enough and that stirrups are down for mounting.
- Give you a great learning experience!

Do

✔ Check the girth is tight enough.

✔ Take time to prepare before mounting.

Don't

✘ Dig your toe into the horse's side as you mount.

✘ Pull the back of the saddle when attempting to mount.

✘ Bang your weight down into the saddle as you mount.

2

Always check your stirrups are the right size for your foot with just a little extra room for movement with the leather laid flat against the leg.

3

The most important pre-mount check is to ensure the girth is secure enough to hold the saddle in place. Don't tighten the girth too suddenly, but tighten it gradually in easy stages.

4

Once the rider is mounted, the instructor will explain what to do and how the lesson will evolve.

Mounting

There are various methods of mounting a horse. Each has its merits, but the two most common are getting on from the ground and getting on from a mounting block. Everyone needs to know how to get on from the ground, as if you are alone and there is nothing to mount from, this is the *only* method!

Mounting a horse can require quite a lot of effort, depending on your physical fitness and the size of the animal. Once mastered, it is a technique that becomes quite easy, but it is important that the horse stands still throughout. All horses should be trained to stand for mounting, but many aren't!

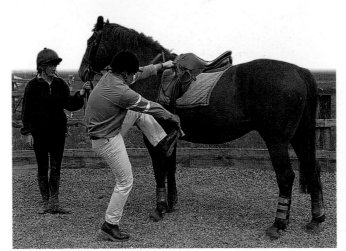

1

Start by facing towards the horse's hindquarters, standing at his shoulder on his near side. Take hold of the reins with your left hand and the stirrup iron with your right. Lift up your left leg and place your foot well into the stirrup iron.

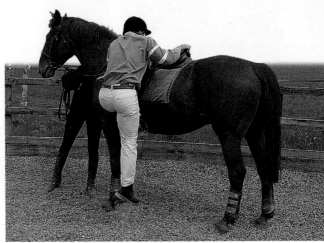

2

Swivel around to face the horse's side and push upwards, taking care not to twist the saddle, easing yourself up and taking your weight on the stirrup iron.

Learning goal
Mounting is certainly one of the more difficult things you have to learn, but with practice it soon becomes relatively easy.

Pre-mounting checks
Before you attempt to mount, check that the girth is tight enough and that the stirrups have been pulled down and are roughly the right length for you. Your instructor should help you to check these things and will hold the horse throughout the mounting session.

3

Lift your right leg high enough to avoid hitting the horse's rump. Your right hand can help to stabilize your weight as you start to settle down into the saddle.

4

Sit down gently in the saddle and find your other stirrup iron either by moving your foot or with the help of your hand. Take up the reins in both hands and think about your position in the saddle.

On board

You must ensure that you are sitting square on the horse. To do this you may need to hold on to the front arch of the saddle and stand up in the stirrups to ensure that they are even and you are sitting square. Your instructor will talk you through this if necessary, while you get used to the feeling of sitting on a horse.

Using a mounting block

Mounting from a block is covered in more detail on pages 74–75, but is based on the same principle as mounting from the ground. Note that it is much easier to mount from a height and it is also kinder to the horse's back, as there is less pull on his spinal muscles.

Do

✔ Talk to your horse when mounting.

✔ Pat him once you have settled into position.

✔ Keep hold of the reins when getting on, so you have control should he move.

✔ Ensure your foot is straight in the stirrup.

✔ Stand up in your stirrups to ensure they are an even length.

Don't

✘ Dig your toe into the horse's side when mounting – push your toe downwards instead.

✘ Pull on the back of the saddle, as this could twist the saddle tree (the metal frame inside the saddle).

✘ Bump down into the saddle as this could frighten the horse or put strain on his back.

The correct position

Once you are up on on the horse, you need to think about your position and what you should be doing, and your instructor will run through each aspect with you.

Breathing

Breathing correctly during your lesson is important. It is surprising how many riders hold their breath while concentrating on what they need to learn. This is not helpful: stay relaxed and breathe normally.

1
The instructor is explaining what is going to take place.

2
The instructor is leading a beginner for his first steps on the horse.

Basic position

• You should sit erect on the horse without being stiff, and look straight ahead.
• Your legs should hang down as long as possible, with your feet resting in the stirrup irons.
• For greater security, your heel should be pushed down and your lower leg relaxed but lightly hugging the horse when moving, to maintain an even contact.
• Your knee should be bent and the stirrup length adjusted to suit: a little too short is generally better than too long at this stage.
• Your arms should hang naturally at your sides with your elbows bent, and your hands should rest just above the wither with your thumbs uppermost.

First steps

Your trainer will go through all this while leading you for a few steps to allow you to get used to the horse's movement. To start with, it is best to lean forward a little rather than back while you find your own balance. Practise starting and stopping a few times, until you have learned how to stay in balance with your horse as he does this.

Your trainer will lead you around on a lunge line until you feel confident and will then give you a long line to walk out on the circle. Try little twists and turns until you gain confidence that you are actually influencing the horse and getting him to do your bidding.

3

Now that the rider is feeling more confident, the instructor has let the horse out on a circle at the end of a lunge line. Note the enclosed pen – ideal for safety and gaining confidence.

4

The rider is coping well, but needs to sit up more and hold his head up, and push a bit more weight down into his heel for added security.

Safety first

Safety must always be the priority and there are no two situations that will be the same. Your instructor will assess each horse-and-rider combination along with other factors such as the weather and your ability to cope with situations as they arise.

Using the reins

Holding the reins correctly will help the horse receive the most direct instructions from you, the rider. Remember that the horse's mouth is naturally very sensitive and the lighter you are with your rein aids the better.

Unfortunately, not all riding school horses are as responsive as they could be, as they have often had numerous riders tugging and pulling at them, so that their mouths have become somewhat insensitive.

Control and steering

Your ability to stop, start and steer can, and should, be the number one priority once you have learnt how to get on the horse.

Learning goal
Practice makes perfect. Keep practising each new-found skill until you feel completely confident that you are communicating effectively with your horse and achieving the right results.

Stopping
Now that you have experienced the horse's movement in walk and have adjusted your balance to go forward in time with him, you will be able to experiment in all sorts of ways quite quickly.

The most important thing of all is to start feeling in control. Your trainer will ask you to stop and start, firstly on the lunge. To ask the horse to stop, take a gentle pull on the reins – just enough to feel the horse responding, then relax your hands. Practise until you feel confident that the horse is listening and responding to your commands, and you know that you can stop him.

1
The most essential aspect of riding is to feel that you are in charge, so learning how to stop and start your horse is vital.

2
The horse reacts to the stimulus from your legs to move forwards and the restriction of your hands on the reins to stop. Practise until you feel confident.

Moving forward
To make the horse move forward you must nudge or kick, if necessary, until you get a response. Always start with a gentle nudge with your heels against the horse's sides just behind the girth. Depending on his response, you may need to be stronger and more insistent until you get the reaction you need. Remember that you will need to relax your hands and allow him to move forward freely. Practise moving forward and stopping around the arena, until you feel that you have mastered this. Your trainer will be happy to let you off the lunge line as soon as you feel confident to go it alone.

1
The rider is trying the trot for the first time and bumping in the saddle whilst maintaining his balance by keeping his weight forward.

2
The rider is now learning to rise out of the saddle in time to the horse changing from one diagonal pair of legs to the other.

Turning
You can practise turning at the same time as stopping and starting. Take a slightly stronger feel on the right or left rein to ask the horse to change direction. To keep the forward momentum, you will need to use both legs on his sides as you turn, otherwise the horse may stop. He needs direction from you as to what you want him to do, so you need to learn to think as he does: 'What does she want me to do now?'

Secret of success
The hands control the horse and the legs ask him to move forward – it is the balance between these two that ensures control of the horse.

Communicating with the horse

After each stage and every new skill you learn, it is always worth stopping and thinking it through. You, the rider, are on top of an intelligent but dumb animal and you are expecting him to understand everything you are trying to tell him, even though at this stage you do not know much about it yourself!

- Be consistent in everything you do and note the response you get from your horse. In this way, you can start to build up a partnership and understanding between you.

- A horse generally learns through repetition. He will have been trained to respond to particular signals, and it is important that his riders recognize this and use similar signals, so that the horse does not become confused.

The walk

Walk sequence
In the walk, the horse lifts and sets down each foot independently, in the following sequence:

1 Left (near) hindleg.
2 Left (near) foreleg.
3 Right (off) hindleg.
4 Right (off) foreleg.

1

Here the left hindleg has taken the weight of horse and rider and is about to push this on to the left foreleg.

2

The left foreleg has now taken the weight and is about to put this on to the right hindleg.

Learning goal
The walk requires a certain amount of freedom from the rider's hands, so that the horse can move his head and neck in an unrestrained way as he changes from one foot to another. Work on moving your hands slightly forward in unison with the horse's stride.

The 'paces' or 'gaits' are terms used to describe the three different ways the horse moves – namely, the walk, trot and canter. On your first day, you will be attempting the walk and trot only. For details on the canter, see pages 90–91.

In all paces, the horse should move confidently forward and go straight. He should be in balance and maintain a good rhythm. In this way, it is much easier for the rider to keep her balance and develop a good position on the horse.

Understanding the walk
So far, you have been learning to ride in walk. It will help you to make progress if you understand exactly how the horse moves his legs and body in walk.

The walk is a 'four-time' pace, with four distinct steps being taken in turn as the horse picks up each foot independently. It should be loose and supple, with the horse moving freely forward and in balance.

3
The right hindleg has already taken the weight and then pushed it on to the right foreleg, ready to begin the sequence again.

4
The rider's hands should move in time with the head and neck movements of the horse in walk.

Do

✔ Keep your horse moving forward.

✔ Allow your hands to move with the natural movement of the horse's head.

✔ Allow your hand to move forward as you turn.

Don't

✘ Lean back, but go with the movement of the horse.

✘ Cross your hand over the neck when turning as it restricts movement.

Types of walk

Free walk The horse moves forward unrestricted, stretching his head down with the rider keeping just enough contact on the bit to help the horse maintain his balance.

Medium walk This walk requires the horse to be more together, with the rider maintaining a contact through the reins and a stronger leg aid.

Collected and extended walks These are more advanced movements, requiring the schooled horse to shorten or lengthen his stride in a more exaggerated way.

The trot

1

As the trot is a two-beat pace, it is easy to see the diagonal pairs of legs on the ground or elevated. Here, the left foreleg/right hindleg pair are on the ground and taking the weight, while the rider rises out of the saddle.

2

The horse extends his stride as the left foreleg/right hindleg pair prepare to leave the ground.

Learning goal
It is the change of diagonal that causes learner-riders difficulty, as they try to master the moment of suspension by rising out of the saddle on every other stride. Once you have understood the up-down, up-down motion required and can do this in time to the horse's movement, the trot is quickly mastered.

The trot is a 'two-time' pace. The horse moves his legs in diagonal pairs, creating the two-beat rhythm, with a moment of suspension as he changes to the opposite diagonal. To be a comfortable ride, the trot should be smooth and supple, not stiff and jarring.

Starting to trot
By now, you will be feeling enough in control on and off the lunge to think of trotting. Your trainer will lead you at this stage, until you have become accustomed to the movement of the trot and learned how to keep your weight forward as the horse's more exaggerated steps throw you upwards.

You can hold on to the neckstrap to help you at this stage. As the horse is asked to trot, keep your weight forward and allow yourself to bounce in the saddle. To start with, ride just a few trot steps at a time, until you feel ready to do more each time. Once you have felt what trotting is all about, have a rest and talk it through with your instructor. You can sit to the trot by allowing

3
The right foreleg/left hindleg pair are now on the ground and taking the weight, while the rider sits in the saddle.

4
The horse steps through as the right foreleg/left hindleg pair push forward, before preparing to leave the ground once again.

Do

✔ Keep your weight forward in this gait.

✔ Go 'with' the horse as he trots.

✔ Find the rhythm of the trot, and rise and sit to this movement.

✔ Maintain your balance and keep your body sitting straight.

✔ Keep your hands low.

✔ If you are trotting too fast, slow the horse down and try again.

Don't

✘ Allow your weight to fall backwards.

✘ Raise your hands and slide your legs forward.

✘ Lose balance and start bumping on the saddle.

✘ Panic if it doesn't work first time – try again.

yourself to bump in the saddle to the horse's movements. Eventually you will be able to soften your back muscles so that you bounce around relatively little.

Learning to rise
When you begin trotting again, work on the co-ordination of using your legs to push you up and down in time with the horse, rising out of the saddle on every other stride. Keep your legs back behind the girth – do not allow them to slide

forwards and your weight backwards. Keep your hands as low as possible at this stage, and try to rise forwards 'over your hands'. Keep your head up and look forward between the horse's ears.

To perfect the art of trotting requires plenty of practice, so use the little-and-often maxim. Keep practising moving from walk to trot and back to walk and then halt. You will soon start to feel confident that you can stay with your horse as he takes you through the transitions between walk and trot.

Common faults

It is very easy to allow bad habits to take over if you are not careful early on. Be sure to take note of comments about your position and ask for help in correcting faults. Everyone has a different body shape, which tends to accentuate faults. The size and shape of the horse you are riding and your current level of confidence are also factors.

The faults illustrated here are very common and easily rectified, but you will need to remind yourself consciously about them on a regular basis.

Learning goal
Listening and learning from your instructor will ensure you avoid getting into bad habits. Looking at photographs or video recordings of yourself can be very useful in understanding any faults you may be developing.

1

Allowing the lower leg to slide forward This is one of the most common faults of all. Once the leg has gone forward in front of the girth, the rider tends to slide backwards, putting too much weight on the back of the saddle and the horse's back. This can result in the rider's hands coming up as balance is lost – the reins (and therefore the horse's mouth) then become the main means of support.

As a general guide, try to achieve a straight line down from your shoulder joint through your hip joint to your heel. This will help to keep you more in balance and better able to influence the horse – he will be relieved that all your weight is not sitting in one area on the back of the saddle. Some saddles, particularly those used for jumping, are very forward-cut and this can accentuate the problem, so a change may make a difference.

2

Collapsing the hip If you do not sit square on the horse and feel each seat bone, it is very easy to allow yourself to collapse your hip on one side or the other. This causes a major distortion of the spine and gives the horse a real problem in maintaining his balance, let alone coping with yours.

Try always to think of sitting square and up straight on the horse, with your hips parallel to his hips and your shoulders following his shoulders. Stand up in your stirrups to ensure that your leathers are of even length and check that the saddle is straight on the horse's back. If it feels uneven to you, talk to your trainer. Keep saying to yourself that you must sit straight to help your horse.

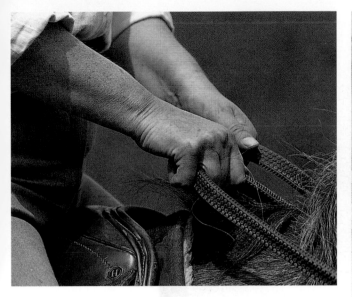

3

Incorrect hand position This rider is holding the reins in the 'pram-pushing' position. Instead, you should hold your hands curved slightly inwards from the wrist and with thumbs uppermost. Your arms should hang relaxed from shoulders to elbows. The muscles will then remain loose and supple for use in any requests your hands need to make to the horse.

You need to keep your hands still, but your fingers need to be flexible and sensitive in order to indicate to the horse when you want him to turn or slow down. It is not a matter of tugging or pulling, but a 'take-and-give' request until you get the response you want. However, in the early stages before your co-ordination on a horse is fully developed, a gentle pull is most likely to work best.

4

Leaning forward with heels up To start with, it is best to keep your weight forward until you have found your balance, especially during transitions forward or when moving off from halt. As you gain in confidence, you can sit up straight and 'go with' the movement of the horse.

Allowing your weight to draw upwards usually results in your toes sliding down and your heels coming up and back. Your legs control the way you ride – they are like the roots of a tree, and strong roots result in a strong overall position. You therefore need to master your leg position early on. Direct your weight down into your heels, which should rest slightly lower than your toes.

Dismounting and untacking

Getting off the horse is relatively straightforward but requires some practice. As with mounting (see pages 50–51), it is important that the horse stands still. As a beginner, your trainer will keep the horse still until you are confident to hold the reins and dismount at the same time.

Learning goal
Running the stirrups up the back of the leathers (see left) is easily achieved with a few practices. It is an important safety precaution that will prevent accidents.

Stirrup safety
Never leave stirrups hanging down when you are not mounted. Instead, run them up the back of leathers and tuck in the ends as shown. The reasons for this are:

- The horse could kick out at a fly and get his foot caught in the stirrup.
- The stirrups could bang against the horse's sides or sensitive elbows.
- The stirrups may get caught in stray twigs or other obstacles as you lead your horse past.

Any of these scenarios could have disastrous results!

1
Keeping hold of the reins, lean forward and start to swing your right leg up over the horse's back.

2
Make sure that you lift your leg high enough not to hit the horse on his rump, which might result in unwelcome consequences!

Dismounting safely

Don't forget to bend your knees when dismounting to absorb the impact.

Preparing to dismount

Bring the horse to a halt and give him a pat as a 'thank you' for your ride. Take your feet out of both stirrups, while maintaining your hold on the reins to ensure that he does not move forward.

Untacking

With the reins over your horse's head, put your left arm through them to keep hold of the horse. To remove the saddle, unbuckle the girth, lift up the saddle and pad (if used), then slide everything towards you. Put the reins back over the horse's head. To remove the bridle, undo the noseband and throatlatch before easing the bridle off over one ear, then the other, allowing the bit to slide gently from the horse's mouth.

Saying 'thank you'

Lead your horse back to the yard after the lesson and untack him. If he is hot, he will appreciate being sponged off, especially where he is sweaty – usually on the neck, under the saddle and around his head where the bridle has been. Use a wet sponge and remove excess water with a sweat scraper.

Lead the horse out to the paddock for a roll and a graze. This is the best reward a horse could have.

3

With both legs now on the same side, lower yourself to the ground. At the same time, control your downward drop by keeping a feel of the saddle and pushing yourself slightly away from it.

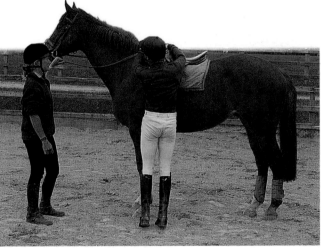

4

Land with slightly bent knees. Now you are safely down, you can release your hold on the reins. Now take the reins up over the horse's head and put up the stirrups, before leading the horse back to the yard.

Reviewing your first lesson

Having now experienced your first ever lesson on a horse, you can sit down and give yourself a pat on the back. As with trying anything new, it has taken quite a bit of thought, pre-planning and a certain courage to accept the challenge. Everyone will have had a slightly different approach and will have achieved different levels. You cannot expect to learn more than the basic principles in a weekend, but you can achieve a surprising amount in just one lesson – especially if you have prepared yourself mentally and physically, and have a good trainer, a suitable horse and the will to learn.

Tacking up
You discovered the names and purpose of various items of equipment, and learned the correct way to put them on the horse.

Mounting
You achieved what is probably the most difficult manoeuvre to master at this stage: actually getting on the horse.

Sitting correctly
You assessed your balance on the horse and learnt how to adjust your position and sit correctly and safely in the saddle on a moving horse. You have learned about common faults and what to do about them.

List your achievements

Looking back over what you have done, you will probably be surprised at how much you have achieved in such a short space of time. You probably feel more breathless just thinking about all you have achieved than when you were actually doing it. You have succeeded in mounting, achieving the correct position, learned how to canter, and may possibly have attempted trotting, and dismounted. Well done!

Control and steering
You learned and practised how to start and stop the horse, and how to turn in different directions. You may even have been allowed loose off the lead rein or lunge to walk the horse around the arena.

Trotting
The more ambitious may have achieved a short trot and felt the effort that needs to be used to sit and rise in time to the horse's movement in this gait.

Dismounting
You learned how to get off the horse and take him back to the yard or field.

Safety checklist

Until you have experienced riding a horse, it is difficult to appreciate how important it is to be sensible and not take risks. To those who have mastered the degree of balance and co-ordination required to stay on a moving animal, while at the same time asking it to perform numerous different procedures, it seems easy. However, no-one achieves this without at some stage encountering those alarming moments when a loss of balance or an unexpected reaction from the horse results in a fall or near miss. It is all part of riding and that slight feeling of risk is just one of its great attractions.

Understanding the horse

You need to understand how a horse thinks and reacts to be able to appreciate how he is likely to react to different situations. Most horses used at riding schools have been specially chosen and trained because of their temperaments and suitability for coping with beginners. While this is wonderful in many ways, it does mean that some animals become rather set in their ways and lose the all-important responsiveness to your commands that makes them easier to ride.

Learning goal

Learn to understand your horse's mentality and react to him. Think ahead and prepare yourself and your horse to respond to various everyday situations.

Safety reminders

There are a number of safety points to bear in mind that will help you throughout your riding career.

- Be consistent. Always ask for something in the same way, so that the horse is able to understand what it is you want.
- Remember that when you ask for a response you must acknowledge this by responding back to the horse. For example, when you ask for a turn to the right and the horse responds by turning right, stop asking. Otherwise he will stop listening to your requests.
- Only ask a horse for what he is physically able to achieve – you cannot push a square plug into a round hole. He may respond with a definite 'no' and you end up creating a problem.
- Think ahead and do not allow dangerous situations to arise in the first place. Assess how to keep out of trouble, then decide what to do and do it.
- Remember that your horse is not a machine to be used or abused. He requires care and attention daily, and a thorough understanding of his needs to keep him healthy and content.
- Treat your horse as you would want to be treated yourself: with respect and fairness. Give him space – he needs his breaks just as much as you need yours. He will get fed up and irritated if you are always fussing.
- Be aware of the safety policy at your riding school and know how to contact the doctor, vet or emergency services, should this ever be necessary.

Ignoring any or all of these points may cause resentment and unwanted behaviour in the horse, which could ultimately have implications for your safety.

1

These riders, who are both wearing back protectors, are having a great time riding through water. Before you enter any water, however, always ensure that it is safe and not too deep.

2

Get to know how your horse reacts to your commands. Is he responsive, sluggish, quick or slow? Once you know his natural instincts, you will be able to gauge his reactions.

Secret of success

It is important to plan ahead. If you really try to do this, you will be far better prepared and able to cope with situations as they arise.

Do

✔ Be consistent.

✔ Ask for advice and help.

✔ Check your hat is secured before moving off.

✔ Check girths are tight.

✔ Pull up if getting out of control.

Don't

✘ Panic if problems arise.

✘ Go faster than you feel is safe.

✘ Allow others to influence you to do things you don't feel ready to attempt.

The tack room

The hub of activity in any yard is usually the tack room. This is where many of the processes that go on begin and end. For example, the tack for your horse will be stored on his own peg, collected from there before your lesson and returned there afterwards.

A typical tack room

Tack rooms vary enormously, but generally the bulk of all equipment for the horses is stored inside. This can include:

- Rugs.
- Grooming kits (see page 27).
- Saddles and bridles.
- Other riding tack.
- Veterinary equipment (usually kept in a special cupboard).
- First-aid kit.
- Tack cleaning kit.
- Telephone and emergency numbers and procedures.
- Yard diary.

In many yards, the tack room may also have tea- and coffee-making facilities – particularly welcome after lessons in colder weather.

A typical tack room showing the saddle horse or rack generally used for tack cleaning. Note the various bridles neatly hung on their pegs after cleaning.

First impressions

Some tack rooms are more functional than others; some are adorned with photos and trophies won by yard stars. Each tack room tells a different story and, to a certain extent, reflects the way the yard is run. However, remember that it is not always the smartest, tidiest and glossiest tack room that indicates whether the horses are well cared for in their stables and paddocks.

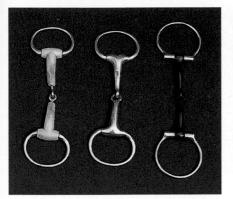

1

Three different types of snaffle mouthpiece (from left to right): plastic-covered, metal and sweet iron.

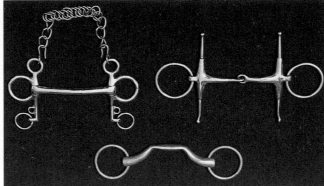

2

Three different bits (clockwise from left): pelham with curb chain, cheek snaffle and shaped snaffle.

3

A general purpose saddle ready to be put on a horse with a white saddle pad. A wooden horse like this one or a metal saddle rack are ideal for storing saddles as they support the shape of the saddle.

Learning goal

It is worth familiarizing yourself with the tack room, so that you know where various items of equipment are stored and why. Most yards have tack for individual horses, and a grooming kit either for each horse or for a group of horses. Naming of kit is important if it is a big yard, as it is vital to keep equipment together that belongs to specific owners or has been put out for certain horses. Learn about the system that your yard operates.

Cleaning tack

One of the most rewarding things you can do at the end of your lesson is to relax and clean your tack. This gives you the opportunity to relive your lesson – and perhaps feel those newly used muscles starting to tell you they have done some work!

Preparation

Hang up the bridle on a peg or tack hook and place the saddle on a saddle horse, ready for cleaning. This enables you to work on the tack easily, cleaning and soaping it thoroughly, ready for use the next day. When you have finished, return the tack to its allocated peg.

Learning goal

Get into the habit of checking your tack to ensure it is soft and supple enough not to rub your horse in any way. Be alert to any signs of stitching coming undone or any deterioration that could compromise your safety.

Most stables have a bridle for each horse kept on its own peg. To keep the tack in good condition, it should be wiped over daily after use and thoroughly cleaned once a week.

Cleaning the bridle

To clean a bridle, first undo the buckles to allow a thorough clean, which is best done at least once a week. Otherwise, simply remove the straps from their keepers.

1 Take a damp sponge or wash rag and briskly rub both sides of the leather clean.
2 Rinse the bit thoroughly, making sure it is clean at the edges and where the rings and mouthpiece meet.
3 With a moist sponge, rub saddle soap well into all parts of the leather.
4 Do up the buckles (or just replace the keepers), then pick up the end of the reins, thread the throatlatch through them and fasten. Fasten the noseband around the outside of the bridle.
5 Dry the bit with a cloth, then replace the whole bridle on its peg.

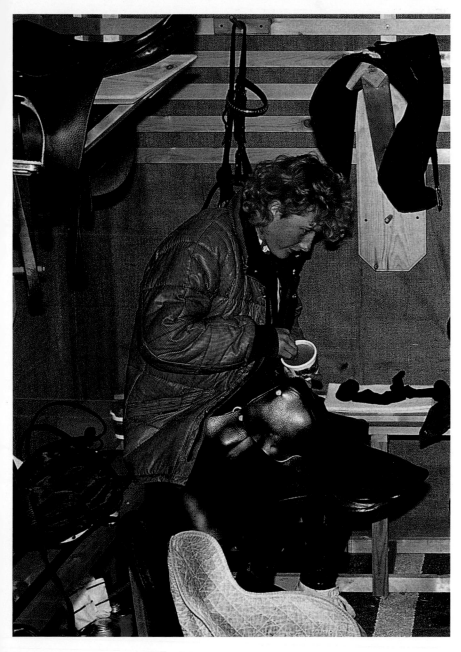

Cleaning the saddle

1 Remove the girth. If it is made from leather, clean and soap thoroughly on both sides. If it is made from a synthetic material, sponge or wipe off as necessary and then hang up to dry and air. Occasionally, use a stiff brush to remove hairs and freshen up the girth.

2 If the saddle is made from leather, take a damp sponge or wash rag and briskly rub both sides of the leather clean, taking care to check under the saddle flaps and girth straps. Lift it upright and clean the underside. With a moist sponge, rub saddle soap well into the top and underneath, paying special attention to the girth straps.

3 Clean the stirrups with a damp cloth and dry them. Clean and soap the stirrup leathers. Once a week, take the leathers right off the stirrup bars and open them up for cleaning and soaping.

4 Place the saddle on its rack. If a saddle cover is used, put this on over the saddle to protect it from dust.

5 If you have a synthetic saddle, occasionally wipe off the dirt and sponge the underside clean if it is heavily soiled.

Safety check

Check the stitching on bridles, girths, stirrup leathers and saddles each time you clean them, and if it appears loose or worn send the item to a saddler for repair.

Saddles are expensive and need treating with care to ensure they are not damaged or dropped. This one is being well soaped after cleaning and will then be placed on a saddle rack.

DAY 2: MAKING PROGRESS

After the success of your first ride, you will be brimming with confidence and ready to do even more. This chapter takes you through new techniques that will enable you to progress, through a logical step-by-step process to suit your ability and ambitions.

Other methods of mounting

Mounting from the ground has already been described in detail on pages 48–49. Every new rider must master this technique, as it will not always be possible to use the easier alternative methods of mounting from a block or receiving a leg-up from another person.

Leg-up

When giving or receiving a leg-up, it is important for you both to agree when you intend to co-ordinate the lift-up. The rider must be ready to spring upwards when indicated and most people do so on the count of three.

Learning goal
Whichever method you choose, practice is the only sure way of becoming proficient.

1
Pull down the stirrups and turn to face the horse's side. Your helper should support your lower leg with both hands.

2
Take up the reins then spring upwards into the saddle on an agreed signal.

3
Swing your leg over the back of the horse, sit down gently in the saddle, then put your feet in the stirrups.

Secrets of success
- Be sure that you spring up high enough to be able to get on to the horse without your leg hitting his back.
- Co-ordination is all-important. If you and your helper do not work together you will end up as a 'dead' weight, which makes for heavy work for both parties.

1

Take up the reins and place your foot in the stirrup. Take care not to dig your toe into the horse's side.

2

Straighten your knee and swing your right leg up.

3

Swing your leg over the horse's back, taking care not to kick him on the rump.

4

Lower yourself gently down into the saddle. Put your foot in the opposite stirrup and settle yourself into position.

Tightening the girth while mounted

Always check the tightness of your girth before moving off.

Ask your helper or trainer to feel the girth for you. Alternatively, take the reins in one hand to hold the horse still, then lean forward and slide your fingers underneath the girth to check that it is tight enough to hold the saddle in place so it will not slide back.

If you need to tighten the girth, take both reins in one hand. With the other hand, lift up the saddle flap and feel first for the front strap. Ease it up a hole, then feel for the back strap and repeat.

Mounting from a block

This method of mounting is possibly the easiest, as you are up in a position where little physical effort is required. Your trainer will be there to guide and help you. Depending on the size of the horse and height of the block, you will usually bring the horse up to stand stationary by the block and then step up yourself.

Vaulting

For the young and athletic, it is possible to vault on to a horse, either when the horse is stationary or when he is moving, as in mounted games. However, this method should only be used by experienced riders whose co-ordination and balance on a horse is well established.

Steering and control exercises

Mastering the art of steering is very important and it is well worth spending a little time at this stage to get the basics properly established before moving on. It is always good to have a plan for what you want to achieve during your lesson and to discuss this with your teacher. This way, you will start to improve in a logical way, getting one thing right before embarking on another.

Circles

There are numerous exercises you can start to work on that will help to build up your muscle power and co-ordination. Circles are the most basic, but require a surprising amount of time and effort to master completely.

It is important to ensure that the exercises are performed on both reins (in both directions) and that you realize that the horse must stay on track. Your outside leg prevents the quarters from swinging out, while the inside leg prevents the horse from falling in on the circle. In an arena, circles are usually ridden in sizes of 20 m (66 ft), 15 m (49 ft) or 10 m (33 ft) in diameter; the smaller the circle the more active and precise you need to be to keep the horse moving.

This rider is learning to ride in a circle around his trainer. When making turns, the outside hand must allow the horse to bend in the direction he needs to follow by being brought slightly forward.

Learning goal

As a beginner, you will need to work on establishing a rhythm with free, forward movement and aim towards performing round circles rather than square ones!

Variations

There are variations of circles in the form of loops, half-circles and serpentines (see right). While all these exercises help the horse to be loose and supple in his work and are used regularly to school the horse, they are also invaluable in helping you, the rider, to be more effective and aware of the influence you need to have on your horse.

Half-halt

The half-halt or half-stop is exactly what it says and is one of the most widely used exercises at all stages of the horse's training. It also helps to develop the rider's co-ordination and effectiveness, and should be practised regularly.

To perform a half-halt at walk or trot, the horse must first be moving forward in a good rhythm. Prepare to halt by sitting up and slowing the horse almost to a stop, then ride him forward again. Paradoxically, it is important to think of this as a forward movement, as it is actually designed to *increase* the impulsion or forward movement of the horse. As you progress, your trainer will use this exercise in all gaits to increase the balance and co-ordination between horse and rider.

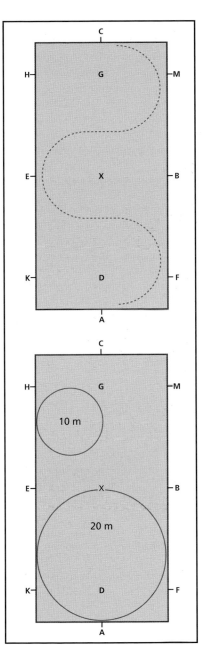

Mastering a serpentine with three loops like this one may take a bit of practice as it can be difficult to make evenly spaced turns.

Circles test the rider's control and use of the aids. The smaller the circle, the more precise the rider's actions need to be.

Checklist

When performing any exercise, it is important to have certain basic thoughts in your mind.

✔ Maintain forward movement, rhythm and balance.

✔ Keep to the correct route through the exercise.

✔ Your shoulders should be square to the horse's shoulders and your hips square to the horse's hips.

✔ Your hands control the balance and steering of the horse.

✔ Your legs influence the speed and control the hindquarters.

The arena

Every riding school has an arena of some description, although some are more sophisticated than others. This may vary from a coned-off area in the corner of a field to a purpose-built 'manège' with a special all-weather surface. Larger riding schools may even have an indoor arena, which is a godsend in bad weather.

Whatever the facilities, the arena is the focal point for riders. Although an arena can be of any reasonable size, many are built to the universally recognized dressage arena sizes. Small arenas are 20 x 40 m (66 x 131 ft), large arenas 20 x 60 m (66 x 197 ft).

M, B and F make up the sequence in a small arena, while in a large arena the letters R, S, V and P are added on either side of these midway markers (see opposite).

There are also markers down the centre of the school. The most important of these is X, which marks the halfway spot in the school and is situated on the centre line between E and B. The letter G, often used as a stopping point in a dressage test, is on the centre line between markers M and H.

Learning goal
When riding in an arena, aim to develop a feel for where the markers are and practise riding from one to another until you can do this accurately.

Arena markers
Around the arena, universally recognized letters are to be found in specific positions. It is worth trying to memorize where these are, so that you have some idea what to do when your trainer starts to ask you to perform a movement at a particular letter.

The entrance, marked A, is centrally placed at one end of the arena and thereafter letters follow clockwise around the arena. The letters K, E, H, C,

Learning your letters
Most people memorize a sentence to remind them of where the markers are positioned around the sides of the arena. You could try:

All King Edward's Horses Can Manage Big Fences (A, K, E, H, C, M, B, F)

Or try making something up yourself, but be sure it corresponds to the correct sequence of letters.

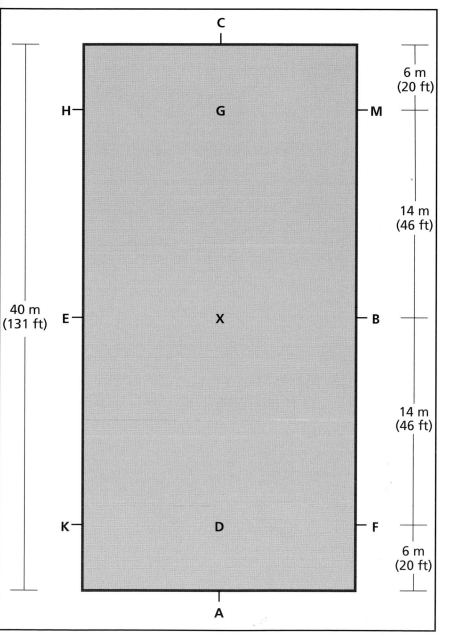

C

6 m
(20 ft)

H — G — M

14 m
(46 ft)

40 m
(131 ft) E — X — B

14 m
(46 ft)

K — D — F

6 m
(20 ft)

A

The small dressage arena is 20 x 40 m (66 x 131 ft) and has standard letters used in all riding arenas. A larger version, 20 x 60 m (66 x 197 ft) is also used and many arenas are even bigger for general riding or jumping use. All dressage tests start by entering at A.

Basic arena terminology

You will need to learn some of the basic terms used in an arena in order to carry out your trainer's instructions accurately.

Change the rein This term denotes a change in the direction in which you are travelling around the school, normally carried out diagonally across the centre.

Track right or left This simply means turn right or left.

Rein back, back up Ask the horse to step backwards, usually for three or four steps.

Go large Continue riding around the arena.

Riding alone

All the activities discussed so far can be carried out on or off the lunge line depending on your progress, confidence and ability, but hopefully you will very quickly have become confident enough to cope on your own, particularly in a confined area.

Practise the basics

There is a wonderful feeling of freedom once you are able to go it alone, but do not get carried away until you have mastered the basics. Practice will make perfect, so build up your confidence by repeating everything you have learned in the arena so far, until you are really sure that you know how to stop, start, steer and keep your balance at both walk and trot.

1

Riding alone for the first time is an exhilarating experience as you realize that you and your horse are now a complete partnership.

2

With increased confidence you will soon be progressing to trotting on your own, which will give you a great feeling of independence.

Secrets of success

In difficult situations:

- Never panic – the horse will immediately sense your concern and become anxious himself.
- Keep calm and talk quietly to the horse.
- If you are not in control, circle the horse until control is re-established, then reorganize.
- Keep trying: if at first you don't succeed, try again!

Broadening your horizons

Once you are safe to do so, you can ride out and about and make sure that you can cope as well in a field as in an arena. Your trainer will advise you on what to do or may even ride with you.

Keeping control

Constantly remind yourself how to stop and start – you need to know that you can do this in all situations to build up your confidence. There are times when, for one reason or another, the horse may move a little more freely than you would like or feel able to cope with. Pull him up by sitting up a little and getting the stop reaction from him as you put pressure on the reins.

If you do not feel in control, pull the horse's head around so that he comes on to a circle – it is then much easier to regain control. Soften your hands as soon as he has stopped, pat him and evaluate the situation.

3

Looking very pleased with himself, this rider has mastered the techniques required to control and steer the horse and is ready to venture out of the arena.

4

On their own and riding confidently down the track on their way back from the lesson – an ambition achieved.

Some common problems

Problem	Suggested solution
Kicking out at flies or your leg.	Sit up and ride forward.
Attempting to buck with head down.	Pull horse's head up sharply, ride forward.
Not going forward.	Loosen reins a little and give a wake-up call by using your legs with greater emphasis.
Going too fast and out of control.	Circle, pull up, re-evaluate and try again with slightly shorter reins.

Difficulty or opportunity?

Inevitably, there will be times when you become a bit anxious about how you are coping. Talk to your trainer about this aspect of your riding – together you can work out a plan for how you should cope with a particular situation. Some horses may have their own little idiosyncrasies that need to be handled in a certain way – learning how to do this will be a great help to you in the future and increase your confidence.

Learning goal

The best way to learn is to face and deal with a variety of situations. The more you attempt and come through successfully, the quicker you will learn to cope with the unexpected.

The aids

The 'aids' is the term used to describe how the rider gives signals or instructions to the horse. As we cannot tell the horse directly what we want, we have to give him clear and unmuddled directions. This is done through the voice, the seat, the legs and the hands, which are known as natural aids.

Consistency in how you give the aids is important; you must also be careful not to confuse the horse by giving him too many signals at one time or, even worse, endlessly nag at him so that he switches off and refuses to respond to any signals at all.

A variety of aids

The horse has certain sensitive areas of his body that the rider needs to utilize to maximum effect.

Mouth The bit is placed in the horse's mouth and the rider uses her hands to control and communicate with the horse through its action. Using just her fingers, the rider can provide very subtle indications to the horse.

Ears The horse can listen to the rider's instructions – many horses learn voice commands very quickly, but because riders are not consistent enough and so many different people use different words, this useful method is often lost. The rider can also see from his ear movement what the horse is thinking (see pages 14–15).

Flank area (horse's sides) This is very sensitive and by touching it with her legs the rider indicates to the horse the degree of speed required.

Back Through her seat, the rider maintains balance and indicates in a more powerful way how she wants the horse to perform.

Learning goal

It is important to know how to use all these aids together to get the best out of our equine friends. As a beginner, it will take time to refine your movements and aids enough to really influence the horse, but with practice and an understanding of what is required you will get there. You will start to recognize the amount of influence you can have on your horse, and how your aids and position in the saddle can help or hinder him.

Applying leg and rein aids

The leg is used as an inward nudge against the horse's flank, for increased impulsion or energy. It is also used to maintain bend, such as when riding a turn.

The hands give rein aids in a 'take-and-give' action and must work independently of each other. The rider's hands should never pull back or restrict, even when slowing down.

(See also pages 110–111.)

The aids are the method of communication between horse and rider as indicated by this picture.

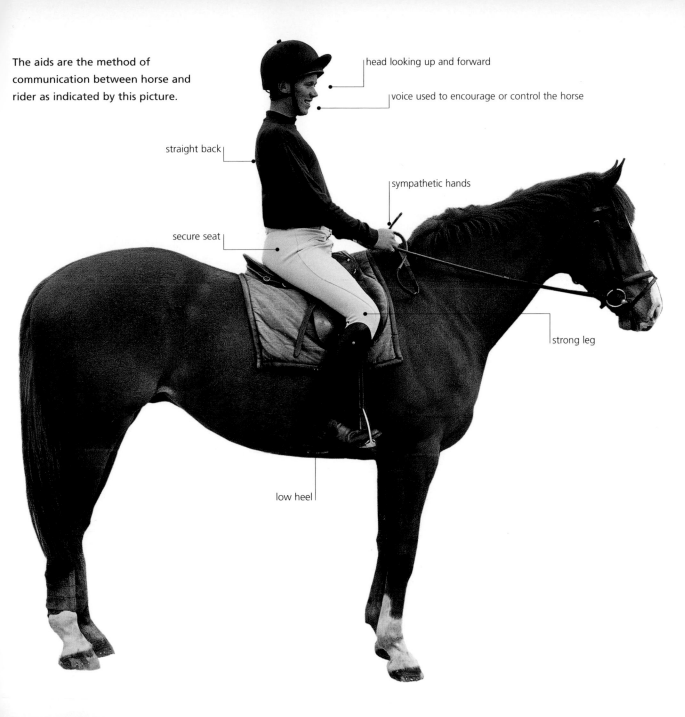

head looking up and forward

voice used to encourage or control the horse

straight back

sympathetic hands

secure seat

strong leg

low heel

Artificial aids

The whip and the spur are known as artificial aids and are used in addition to the natural aids.

Spurs should not be used by beginners, as any loss of balance will result in misuse, but later on they become a useful aid towards greater impulsion and refinement.

The whip, which comes in various lengths and designs, can be used by novice riders to back up a leg aid or if the horse is unresponsive. It should never be used to inflict pain or in temper.

(See also pages 108–109.)

Balance exercises

The movement of the horse requires you, the rider, to be very agile and adaptable in the saddle, as you learn to cope with the different situations you come up against each time you ride. Exercises on the horse can help to improve your balance and co-ordination, which in turn will boost your confidence.

Expect the unexpected

The horse – whether young or old, 'green' or an experienced campaigner – rarely reacts in quite the same way twice, so it is important that you are aware of this and are sufficiently versatile to be ready for the unexpected.

A bird flying out of a tree or a dog barking will spark some sort of reaction in even the quietest horse. It may be an almost imperceptible tightening of the muscles or a slight movement sideways, or it could be much more sudden and reactionary, so the rider needs to be as well prepared as possible.

Learning goal

The best way to learn and increase your confidence is to face and deal with a variety of situations. The more you attempt and come through successfully, the quicker you will learn to cope with the unexpected.

1

Toe touches With your trainer holding the horse's head, place the reins on his neck and sit straight in the saddle. Then lean forward and reach down with you left hand to touch your right foot. It may take a little time for you to relax enough to do this, so don't force yourself. Try to keep your weight central for as long as possible, until you can feel down towards your foot. Sit up gradually, then relax. Repeat the whole exercise on the other side. Depending on how easy or difficult you find this, your trainer will ask you to repeat it at least twice on each side. When you have finished, sit up straight and relax.

2

Arm movements Sitting relaxed in the saddle, raise one arm above your head as high as you can and count to three, taking care not to poke your head forward. Bring it down again and repeat with the other arm. Next, take your arm out sideways and forwards three times on each side and relax. Finally, bring both hands up and then back to touch your shoulders, sideways and then back to touch your shoulders, forwards and then back to touch your shoulders. When you have finished, relax your arms down by your sides.

3

Body swings Hold both arms out sideways and rotate your body from the waist to the right, swinging your arms around as far as you feel confident, then rotate back. Repeat to the left. Do the exercise two or three times in each direction, then relax. It is important to maintain a correct lower leg position – do not allow your leg to slide forward.

Safety first
Never practise exercises on the horse without your trainer or a knowledgeable person holding your horse's head. Choose a quiet and safe environment in which to practise.

Riding outside the arena

Once you feel confident in the arena and can stop, start and turn your horse, you will want to get out and about. Take it a step at a time: each time you do something different you will gain in confidence, knowing you have accomplished this on your own.

Riding out in company

Your first ride outside the arena will probably be with your trainer or someone from the riding school and on a known route that is straightforward and safe. Ideally, you should be accompanied by a person who is aware of your capabilities. This should be someone who does not take risks, but builds up your confidence and encourages you to lead the way where it is suitable and safe to do so. When you feel more capable, you can ride out with friends.

Stay aware

You must learn to think ahead and prepare for having to move off a track or keep in to the side of the road if a car is coming. Adjust your balance when going up or down a hill: lean forward as you go up and lean back a little as you go down (see pages 104–105). Speed plays a part: keep it slow until you feel enough in control to regulate how fast you go.

Riding in woods can be fun if there are good tracks through them, but be aware of low branches – you will need to lean forward far enough to ensure you fit underneath. Stop and evaluate the situation, and stay in walk if necessary. Look out for tree roots, which can cause the horse to trip.

Keep practising

When riding out on a hack, you can practise some of the lessons you have learned in the arena. These can include stopping and starting when it is safe to do so, and even some of the arm exercises shown on pages 84–85 (remember to take the reins in one hand).

Learning goal

Practise using your legs so that you really achieve a reaction forward from your legs aids. They must build up strength to be effective. A stick can be used to provide an extra incentive if you fail to get enough response.

Carry a whip

It is helpful to carry a whip when riding out, as the horse may need to be encouraged forward, especially if he decides he doesn't like something up ahead. Your leg aids will be relatively ineffective at this stage, so use the whip behind your leg as a back-up.

Road safety

If you are riding on the road, you will need to be aware of the motorist's code for your country and the hand signals to use if needed (see pages 100–101).

Riding down slopes requires caution so that the horse is able to balance himself and the rider and adjust to a sensible speed for their level of experience.

Avoiding problems

Always be aware of potential problems when out riding.

If conditions are icy or slippery it is better to avoid the roads if at all possible. If you are caught out by ice, take your feet out of the stirrups and cross them over the pommel of the saddle. This will help the horse to find his own balance without you interfering and will ensure that if he slips over you can quickly lift your legs up to avoid being rolled on.

If riding early or late in the day, or in foggy conditions when visibility is poor, use a reflective tabard and/or bands (see pages 100–101). Be seen, be safe.

If the horse is startled by something on the side of the road or from a hedge, he will shy away from it and into the road, towards the traffic. Try to prevent this happening by inclining the horse's head away from the traffic or carrying your stick, if you are using one, on the side of the traffic (see pages 100–101).

Changes-of-direction exercises

One of the best ways to improve your ability and become an effective rider is to do exercises involving changes of direction. To do this you have to use your legs and hands together – it sounds easy but can take quite a lot of practice to get it right.

Riding a turn

Generally, to change direction you indicate to the horse the route you wish to take by taking a stronger feel on the rein and keeping him moving forward through use of your legs. The left leg should be applied a little more strongly and is used behind the girth, to prevent the horse's hindquarters from swinging out. For a right turn, use the opposite aids.

Learning goal

Your hands control the direction in which the horse moves. Your legs keep him going forward. They also ensure that his hindlegs follow the tracks of his forelegs and do not swing outwards or inwards. Your aim is to learn to use your hands and legs together to produce smooth and accurate changes of direction.

1

This rider is using two barrels to ride between as he changes direction. Notice how his legs are against the horse and he is starting to encourage the horse to turn to the left by taking a stronger feel on the left rein.

2

This time the rider is taking the horse through jump standards. He is using his legs to keep the horse moving forward and is making an obvious attempt to ask the horse to go around the standard to the left, by taking his hand outwards in the direction he wants to go.

Secret of success

When working on these exercises, keep the messages to your horse simple and practise regularly.

Be consistent

Being consistent and definite with your aids to the horse will make all the difference, and will ensure he is able to respond in an equally consistent way. While everyone will do things slightly differently, the basic aids should be the same – whether given by a complete beginner or an experienced professional. It is therefore important to the horse that all riders are taught in broadly the same way.

3

Here the trainer is explaining how to really influence the messages given to the horse, to help him understand what is being asked. The better schooled the horse, the quicker he will respond to the rider's aids.

Practice exercises

There are many different ways of practising changes of direction including the following:

- **Changing the rein** (see pages 78–79) between the markers in the school.
- **Riding half-circles or loops** back on to the track in the opposite direction.
- **Riding up and down the central line** and changing direction or turning across the school and changing on to the other rein.

However, you can also take the opportunity to do something a little different. Make use of barrels or other suitable items, such as jump standards (without the poles), to ride through or around. It helps to concentrate your mind if you have to ride around obstacles that are set out in a variety of different positions.

The canter

Cantering is your ultimate aim for your weekend course. To achieve this will be a great accomplishment of which you can be justifiably proud – and it is a feeling you won't forget.

1
Here the rider is plainly using his right leg to encourage his horse forward and maintain the canter.

2
As the horse stretches forward into his stride, the rider has allowed his hand to stretch forward a little with the movement.

Canter sequence

When the horse is on the right lead, he will move his legs in the following sequence:

- Left hindleg.
- Left foreleg and right hindleg together.
- Right foreleg.
- Moment of suspension.

Understanding the canter

The canter is a 'three-time' gait, in which there are three distinct beats followed by a moment of suspension when all four feet are off the ground.

In canter, the horse uses what is described as a 'leading leg'. This depends on whether he is cantering to the right or the left: when moving to the right, the horse will be on the right lead; when moving to the left, he will be on the left lead.

Aids for the canter

First make sure that the horse is moving forward well in trot. To canter to the right, as the horse approaches a right-handed corner ask him for a bend to the right by gently pulling on the right rein. Then brush your outside leg back and nudge the horse strongly behind the girth, while sitting safely in the saddle. A responsive and well-trained horse should strike off directly into canter. To canter to the left, reverse the aids.

Cantering 'disunited'

A disunited canter happens when the canter sequence is broken and the horse is on the one lead in front and on the other behind, resulting in a very uncomfortable feeling for the rider.

3

The horse is now at the end of the stride and the rider's weight is coming more upright in readiness for the horse to rebalance to make the next stride.

4

Here the horse is almost back in the same position as the first picture ready to repeat the process.

Do

✔ Move your body in unison with the movement of the horse.

✔ Ensure your reins are not too long, otherwise you will be in danger of losing control and balance.

Don't

✘ Lean too far forward or too far back.

✘ Grip upwards out of the saddle with your legs – instead, sink down into the saddle and relax your back.

Learning goal
Once the horse has moved into canter, your aim is to allow your body to move forward in rhythm with the horse's movements. Cantering is a very comfortable gait for the rider, once the necessary balance has been mastered.

Galloping
A faster version of the canter is described as a 'gallop'. The strides become so extended that the sequence is broken and four hoofbeats can be heard, making this a 'four-time' gait. Galloping is for more advanced riders and is beyond the scope of this weekend course.

Pole work

The progression to pole work is an exciting step as it is the start of the road towards jumping. It also helps you to build up confidence and overcome any apprehension about poles or how a horse may react to them. Cantering over poles is one of the best ways of getting a feel for what jumping is all about.

Learning goal
There are numerous different ways of using poles on the ground. They are a useful tool in helping to school the horse and improve his balance and co-ordination – but they are equally effective in helping the rider to do the same. This is your aim when riding these exercises.

1
This rider is circling the horse around a pole on the ground. This is a simple way of using poles to improve your effectiveness and co-ordination.

2
This time the rider is walking the horse over the pole, rather than going around it. The horse must make a little more effort to step over the pole. In trot, even more precision is required on the part of the rider to steer the horse.

Line of poles
A good way to start is with a line of poles, spaced approximately 3 m (10 ft) apart. With this spacing, the horse is able to take one stride between each pole in trot. Circling over, around or through the poles will help to improve your co-ordination and effectiveness as a rider.

Single poles
Single poles placed on the ground in various different positions around the arena can be very useful as a steering exercise. Practise taking the horse over one pole and then riding on to another. This is the start of the process of learning to ride a course of jumps.

So, think of the poles as jumps and try to ride them as a course. Work out the best route through them to give the horse an easy run.

3

Halting between poles requires a more refined control and degree of co-ordination to be successful. This exercise really encourages the rider to be assertive and the horse to be responsive.

4

Here the rider has been doing a serpentine exercise (see pages 76–77) around the end of each pole. This is a suppleness exercise for the horse and helps the rider to co-ordinate the use of hands and legs.

Secret of success
Keep your horse balanced by sitting up and riding him forwards over the poles.

Do

✔ Practise working over the centre of each pole to improve your accuracy.

✔ Remember that working over poles is strenuous for the horse so only practise each exercise three or four times.

✔ Check everything is secure and in place before mounting.

Don't

✘ Increase your speed over the poles to maintain a rhythm.

✘ Allow your balance to get behind the horse's movements – keep upright.

Co-ordination exercises

Now that you have learned so much in the arena and feel secure riding outside, it is fun to work in pairs – two of you riding together and practising different exercises. It requires a little thought and preparation to ensure that you do not have a collision, but in this way you will learn to appreciate the amount of space required to perform different movements.

Learning goal

By riding together, you have to learn to be at a certain place at a certain time. If you ride in pairs, you will have to appreciate each other's position and learn to speed up or slow down to remain with your partner.

1

These riders are changing the rein from opposite directions and will cross over the centre line in the middle of the arena. Practise at walk to start with. Watch your partner and try to meet up and cross over the centre line reasonably close together. You need to be clear who is the leader and who will pass across first to avoid any confusion. Think ahead and speed up or slow down as necessary.

2

Learning to ride to a certain spot is a good exercise in co-ordinating your movements to speed up and slow down.

3

Here one rider is crossing over in front of the other as they change direction across the school.

Start slowly

To start with it will seem quite difficult, but you will soon be able to work together and will be more effective with your aids when you need to stay closer together. By attempting the exercises in walk to start with, you will get the feel of what is necessary and how to perform the movements required. There are many exercises from which to choose, so always try to be clear on what is expected of you.

Working together

Teamwork is a great way to learn to work together – not just with your horse, but with your riding partner as well.

Do

✔ Give each other enough space.

✔ Ride left hand to left hand when approaching another rider in an arena.

✔ Think ahead and prepare for what is to come.

Don't

✘ Squash your riding partner against the arena fence.

✘ Get ahead of, or behind, your partner if you are due to meet up at a certain spot.

✘ Stop practising until you get it right!

4
Riding and keeping together in pairs requires a bit of teamwork, so think ahead and be aware of where your partner is at any time.

5
Following in single file is relatively easy, but try to maintain the same distance between each horse.

6
Riding in pairs is a favourite exercise and these two are walking down the centre line nicely close together. It is not as easy as it looks and requires a bit of practice, especially when trotting, to ensure you negotiate the turn on to the centre line successfully.

Having fun

Now that you are capable of working in an arena with another horse and rider (see pages 94–95), if you enjoy competing it is fun to try some games to develop your ability to compete against your riding partner. All sorts of games can be played on horseback and many can be set up very easily. For details of more advanced mounted games, see pages 140–141.

First game: bending

Bending in and out through a line of barrels or jump standards is a good basic game with which to start. Each rider has their own line down which to ride. You start at one end and set off at a signal from your trainer, bending in a different direction around each barrel until you reach the other end or turn around and come back down the line to the beginning. The first to finish is the winner.

Pony Club games

For children, mounted games and gymkhana races are often the highlight of their horsey lives. If there is a Pony Club branch near enough to join, they will really benefit from the opportunity of taking part in organized mounted games.

The Pony Club is a worldwide youth organization with branches spread around each country. It teaches everything from horsecare and riding to games and competitions.

Being able to lead another pony is an essential skill in competitions – it's not always easy controlling the two.

Ride and lead

Riding one horse while leading another becomes quite an important skill when practising for games. It also teaches you independence and co-ordination with the use of your hands.

It is usual to lead from the left side and hold your reins in the right hand. This is a skill that takes some practice to master and should only be done at the walk until you feel confident. It is important only to practise this with suitable horses or ponies that do not kick.

A choice of games

- Many games make use of music (see pages 120–121). Musical poles, musical chairs and musical sacks are obvious choices.
- Flag races – in which flags from one spot are picked up and taken to another, until all have been transferred – are always popular.
- Precision games are also fun and help your riding skills. There are many different types, but most involve having to carry something such as apples, mugs of water or large balls to somewhere. You must be able to control your mount while holding the equipment in your free hand.

Learning goal

Think up variations on simple themes – such as getting off to pick something up or leading the horse to a certain spot – and practise them. All the games will require effort of some sort and a degree of competitiveness, to enable you to co-ordinate your recently learned skills and compete against your partner.

Games around the world

Different countries have developed different skills according to their local cultures.

Barrel racing and **pole bending** are very popular in western America, with some races run against the clock. In Australia, the **stake race** is particularly popular. All these sports involve some type of bending.

Tent-pegging, which involves the rider using a lance to pick up a wooden peg, is very popular in countries such as Australia, Canada, Egypt, South Africa and Zimbabwe. Both adults and young riders take part.

Hacking out

Hacking out is one of the highlights of riding. There is no better way to enjoy the countryside than from the back of a horse: you are able to appreciate what is going on so much more, and can peer over hedges and walls to see what is happening all around. You also seem less intimidating to birds and animals when on a horse, and these creatures will come much closer than they would if you were in a car or on foot.

Learning goal

You can continue to put many of the exercises and skills you have learned in the arena to good use on your rides, and will be amazed at how much you have achieved so far without really appreciating it. Repeat these exercises regularly while out hacking around the countryside – a more challenging situation than the arena – to enhance your skills further.

Road riding

Always ride safely on roads, be aware of the dangers and stay alert (see pages 100–101).

Beware of riding on grass verges unless you are sure they are safe. They may be littered with broken bottles and other debris thrown out by uncaring drivers, which can pose a real danger to horses.

1

Riding along tracks is a great way to start riding outside the confines of an arena. It teaches you to cope with unexpected events, such as the horse shying away from a bird or a shadow.

Alone or in company?

Never ride out alone until you are experienced enough to do so. Ideally, having someone with you at all times is the safest option in case you have an unexpected accident.

Get permission

Visit landowners and ask for permission to ride on their land. This way you will build up a good relationship with them, which is well worth developing – not all riders are as considerate as they might be.

2

Respect the countryside: always ride in single file around the edge of growing crops.

Safety first
If you are riding in the evening or early morning, or in poor light conditions, use a reflective tabard to ensure that you can be seen. Stirrup lights are a useful addition if you often ride in poor light (see pages 100–101).

Respect the countryside
• Always shut gates.
• Never gallop across fields in which livestock are grazing.
• Walk around the edges of fields with growing crops and, if possible, avoid these altogether until after harvest.

Opening gates

1 Start by positioning your horse alongside the gate and lean over to unfasten the catch – not always easy. Maintain your balance by not leaning so far that you feel vulnerable.

2 Push the gate open wide enough so that there is plenty of room for you to walk through, and make sure that it does not swing back and hit the horse.

3 Turn the horse so that you can push the gate back to secure it and ride up to stand beside it, so that you can do this safely. Check that the gate is fastened properly before moving away.

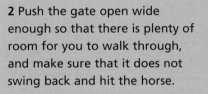

Road safety

Riding on the roads is something to be avoided if at all possible, except on the quieter lanes. However, most people have little option. When riding on the roads, it is important to observe the motorist's code for your country and ensure you do not inconvenience drivers.

Basic rules

- Always keep to the side of the road.
- Be polite and thank drivers who slow down for you. Remember that they will not be able to see your acknowledgement until they are past you.
- Wave drivers past if the road is clear.
- Do not ride more than two abreast at any time. If the road is narrow, stay in single file.
- The less-experienced riders should stay on the inside (furthest from the traffic).

Learning goal

The more you can go out and about, the better it will be for building up your own confidence. It is only by meeting and tackling different situations, such as tucking yourself into a gateway to allow traffic to pass, that you learn to think ahead. Always remember to acknowledge and thank considerate drivers.

1

Do not hog the middle of the road: keep to the side for your own safety.

2

When riding out on narrow lanes, keep in single file to allow room for drivers to pass.

Stay alert

Always be alert and aware of what is going on when riding on the roads. It is irresponsible to be chatting away, oblivious to a build-up of traffic behind you.

Be safe, be seen

Reflective gear is essential if you are likely to be riding in poor light. Drivers will be travelling much faster than you are and in poor light conditions may not see you until the last moment. It is very irresponsible to be out riding without being sure you can be seen clearly.

Use a stirrup light (fitted to the outside stirrup) and fit reflective leg bands on the horse's legs – he could even wear a reflective sheet. These items really show up in the dark and will ensure that you can be seen.

Dusk turns into night very quickly, especially in the winter months, so plan ahead and do not ride too far from base unless you are sure you can get back safely before dark.

3

Ride with at least one horse's length between you, in case a horse is startled or kicks out.

4

These riders are wearing reflective tabards, in case they get back in the dark after their long ride.

Slippery surfaces

Some roads can be very slippery, making it difficult for the horse to keep his feet. Avoid roads like this if you can, or ask your farrier to use anti-slip nails or studs to help. If your horse does slip, loosen the reins and take your feet out of the stirrups so that you can remove your legs out of the way if he slips over, to allow him to regain his balance unimpeded.

Hand signals

It is important to know the basic hand signals used to indicate to drivers what you intend to do (check these with your national equestrian body). Give these in plenty of time and check that drivers behind you understand what you intend to do.

Avoiding problems

A quiet, tranquil scene can quickly become a horror story if you do not anticipate certain situations and take evasive action. Avoid situations that could upset your horse and remember that he can be frightened easily, however quiet he may be. Noisy air brakes are terrifying to many animals, as is wildly flapping canvas on the back of a truck, clattering trailers and many other hazards.

- Turn into a gateway or stop and use hand signals to slow traffic, then turn your horse's head away from the problem.

- Assess each situation as it arises. In some instances, for example when confronted with a herd of animals, it may be better to stop and turn your horse towards the source of alarm.

- When riding in single file, allow at least one horse's length between you and the next rider to prevent overcrowding or risk of kicking.

Weather conditions

The weather can make an enormous difference to your riding activities and it is always worth being prepared. A little thought beforehand will ensure that you are not caught out, and that you and your horse are able to cope with the minimum of inconvenience.

Heat

If it is very hot, your horse is going to sweat a lot and become thirsty – and you will probably suffer in much the same way! Remember, too, that the ground may well be hard and slippery.

Have a washing-down kit – consisting of a bucket of water, sponge and scraper – ready for your horse when you have finished your ride. Offer him water to drink as well, but allow him just one quarter of a bucket at a time until he has cooled down.

Rugs

Make sure that your horse is appropriately rugged for the weather. Keeping him too hot is as bad as him being too cold.

1

Slopping around in these wet conditions makes it virtually impossible to keep really clean for this show class at Palm Beach in Florida.

Cold

In very cold weather, wrap up warmly with suitable clothing and remember that your toes and fingers will feel like blocks of ice in no time at all. Warm socks and gloves are a must, and something to keep your ears warm will make a big difference to your comfort.

An unclipped horse is generally fine ridden as he is, but care must be taken that he does not become chilled after exercise. It is better to turn him out again straight away, so that he can generate his own heat by moving around, rather than keep him standing still in a stable. If he is stabled, a light rug that wicks away moisture would be ideal. A clipped horse can be ridden in a paddock sheet to keep him warm and will require warm rugs after exercise.

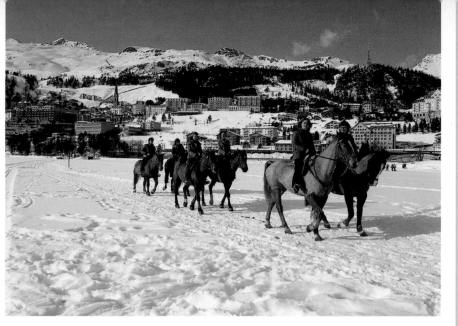

2

Snow shoes, showing the pads and stud holes for grip. If you do not have pads, greasing the soles of your horse's hooves has a similar effect.

3

Riding in snow is fun, but it is important to ensure that the snow does not 'ball' in the feet and cause the horse to slip dangerously.

Riding in slippery conditions

Riding in wet weather is likely to be unpleasant. In addition, the ground may be very slippery and therefore quite dangerous.

- If you are in a group, give each other sufficient room to avoid too much splashing.

- For competitive work, studs put into the horse's shoes will help to control slipping.

- Otherwise, it is best to ride with caution and allow more time for cornering and turns.

Wet

Wet weather is probably the most miserable of all for riding. There is a vast array of wet-weather gear available for both horse and rider, but bear in mind that most rubberized, waterproof kit does not 'breathe'. However, many modern fabrics are breathable, so it should be easy for you to come well prepared for the worst of the weather with jacket and leggings to envelope you from top to toe. Your horse can also wear a waterproof rug, or be scraped down and rugged appropriately after exercise.

Snow

Snow presents its own problems, but these will be reduced by using special snow shoes with pads, which prevent a build-up in the hooves. They also contain a special metal called borium, added for extra grip in the conditions.

Going up and down hills

Riding up and down hills becomes important once you start feeling confident enough to want to ride outside as, unlike the flat surface of the arena, the countryside will inevitably undulate.

Learning goals

Your balance changes depending on the degree of slope up or down and it is important that you learn to feel confident enough to adapt to this both ways. Simply, you need to lean forward to stay in balance when going uphill and sit more upright as you ride downhill. Most people have pushed a wheelbarrow around their garden up and down slopes and it is the same principle – you push and lean forward uphill and brace yourself for the downward descent.

If you are planning a riding holiday (see pages 138–139), it is highly likely that you will encounter more than a few steep descents, as one of the attractions of such holidays is the stunning countryside. Be ready for this by practising beforehand.

Check your brakes

Maintaining an even pace over undulating terrain is beneficial to the horse. Keep your horse controlled by ensuring that your reins are short enough to be effective and that you are able to contain him at the speed you want. Are your 'brakes' really good enough, or do you need to consider a different bitting arrangement when riding outside the arena? Many horses are fine in an enclosed space but feel they can take charge when outside. This can usually be rectified by using a different bit or more effective noseband.

As you did in the arena, practise stopping occasionally on your rides just to make sure that you can! If your horse sticks his head up when you try to stop, it may indicate that you need a martingale and/or that you should refine your natural aids.

Slippery slopes

In slippery conditions, such as when riding up or down hill in the mud, remember to allow the horse enough freedom to use his head and neck as a balancing aid. Hanging on to him too tightly may impede his ability to keep his balance. It is sensible to slow down in slippery conditions to give the horse a better chance of coping with the conditions.

Downhill safety

Some horses get a little excited when out on a ride and tend to put their head down for a buck going downhill. Sit up and jerk the horse's head up for safety.

Making hills easy

Trotting up long hills is less strenuous for the horse and therefore better than walking and sitting down on his back. You may like to stay forward, up out of the saddle, to avoid your weight being on your horse's back – hang on to the mane or neckstrap to ensure you keep your balance.

1

Riding up hills requires you to shift your weight forward. You can see how this horse is pushing with his hindlegs and engaging his hocks to help propel him uphill.

2

When going downhill, your weight comes back and allows the horse freedom of the forehand, so that he can pick his way down. The steeper the slope, the slower you need to go. You must remain in balance and control the speed – which in most cases should be slow.

Safety first
It is very important to tell your trainer if you do not feel secure riding over more challenging terrain, so that you can slow down to a pace you feel more comfortable with.

Different bits and bridles

Every horse-and-rider combination will exhibit a different degree of control, which may vary from adequate to marginal to inadequate. As you progress towards greater independence, it becomes increasingly necessary to ensure that you are as safe as possible and have adequate control.

Rider control

Control very much depends on whose hands are at the end of the reins.

Individual control

There are numerous different bits (see also pages 68–69) to help with the control of the horse, but it is sometimes quite difficult to find the right one for a particular horse-and-rider combination. Some riders will cope well when using a certain bit on a certain horse, while others will not find it so easy.

'Less is best'

As a rider, you need to understand the complexities of different bits, many of which have quite subtle actions and require sympathetic usage. 'Less is best' generally works in most cases, but for the beginner control is vital and 'less' may not be sufficient for that person at that stage of their education.

Learning goal

To understand how different items of tack work, you need to watch a variety of ridden horses so that you start to see the different uses and effects they have on a horse. Always ask a knowledgeable person to explain why a horse is wearing a certain bit or noseband.

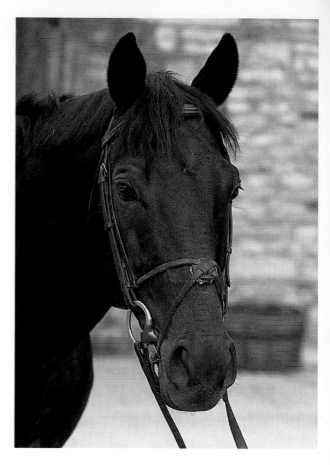

1

This horse is wearing a copper eggbutt snaffle, which is a mild, kind bit. Copper is a soft metal and many horses go kindly in it. The cross-over or grakle noseband is specifically designed to prevent the horse from crossing his jaw, which would make the bit ineffective. The crossed straps fasten above and below the bit, and the cross-over point is covered with sheepskin to ensure comfort.

Nosebands

Choice of noseband can make a big difference. There are four basic types:

- **Cavesson** Fits about the bit approximately 2 finger-breadths below the cheekbone, but inside the cheek pieces of the bridle.

- **Drop** Fits so that it fastens just below the bit.

- **Flash** A combination of both of the above.

- **Grakle or figure-of-eight** A specially designed noseband which prevents the horse dropping his jaw.

Nosebands work by preventing the horse from opening his mouth and resisting, or crossing his jaw. Once the horse uses these methods of evasion, control tends to be lost and only an experienced rider will be able to re-establish it.

2
This horse is wearing a loose-ringed German snaffle, a popular and kind bit, with a flash noseband. This is a combination of the cavesson with a strap fastened through a loop on the front of the noseband, which then goes around the back of the chin under the bit. It prevents the horse from opening his mouth to evade the action of the bit.

3
This horse is wearing a double bridle, generally used for more advanced work such as dressage or for show classes. The bridle has two separate bits, which act independently. A small snaffle, called a 'bridoon', is held slightly higher in the mouth. The second bit is a more severe curb and has a curb chain that dictates its degree of severity. When correctly adjusted, this should be at a 45-degree angle to the mouth. A cavesson noseband, as shown, is the only noseband used with a double bridle.

Whips and spurs

Whips and spurs (see also page 83) are classed as artificial aids and are used to refine and accentuate the use of the legs.

Correct use

While not appropriate until you have mastered the basics, whips and spurs do have their place when used correctly. They should never be used in temper or to abuse a horse – such behaviour is totally unacceptable in our society. They may, however, be used to correct a horse at an appropriate time, to achieve a more refined indication to the horse to go forward or to ask for increased activity.

Whips

There is a variety of whips that can be used, but the most common are:

General-purpose whip A short, straight whip used in everyday riding as an artificial aid to encourage the horse forwards, if necessary.

Dressage or schooling whip A long, thin whip which can be used to activate the horse's hindlegs.

Show cane A straight cane or leather-covered stick, used for showing either in hand or ridden. It may vary in length from a short cane of about 60 cm (24 in) to a fairly long stick, such as that used by side-saddle riders to help compensate for the lack of leg on one side of the horse.

Hunting crop This has a specially designed handle to assist in opening and shutting gates.

Using the whip

To use the whip effectively, take your hand off the rein and encourage the horse forward with a sharp smack of the whip behind your leg. It is important that you do not then lose balance and catch the horse in the mouth with the reins when he responds. To start with, it may be easier for you to tap the horse on the shoulder with the whip.

Spurs

Spurs come in a variety of types, varying from those that have no shank at the back (these are known as 'dummy spurs') to those with a longer shank, including some with rowels as seen in cowboy dress.

Spurs are correct wear in dressage and show classes where long, black boots are used, but should only be worn by those who are in control of their own balance. They are not for beginners.

The whip should rest lightly in the palm of your hand with your fingers curled around it. The wrist action will allow it to be used as necessary.

Using spurs

Strap on spurs with the shank pointing downwards and to the rear. The buckles on the spur straps should be placed just above the slots on the metal and always on the outside. To apply the spurs, turn your toe out very slightly and bring the spur into contact with the horse's flank with a light nudge. Never use the spur on every stride, as this will simply deaden the horse's reaction. Keep your toes pointing forwards, except when a reaction is required from the horse.

Learning goal

It is important to know how to hold a whip and how to change hands with it once you feel confident enough to do so.

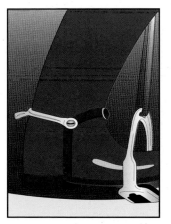

Spurs are a useful aid to achieving a more refined reaction to the leg. They should not be used by beginners.

Moving the whip from hand to hand

You may sometimes need to ride with the whip in a certain hand, to help guide the horse past traffic or something that has spooked him. To transfer a short whip from one hand to the other, take both reins in the hand holding the whip. With the other hand, pull the whip slowly upwards until it is clear of the hand holding the reins, then take the reins back into both hands.

With a longer whip, swing it slowly through 180 degrees in an arc in front of you and over the horse's neck, then take hold of it with the opposite hand. Take care not to frighten your horse when doing this and only do so when standing still.

Improving your technique

Once you have mastered the basics and feel thoroughly confident that you can control your horse, you can start to think about improving your technique. The action of and reaction to certain aids is what is important, so it is now worth considering in a little more detail how each of the natural aids (see pages 82–83) really work and influence what is happening.

Learning goal

The way the legs, hands and seat work together and the co-ordination between all three is the secret of success in riding. Your aim is to develop and improve this co-ordination throughout your riding career.

Legs

The legs are generally considered as the accelerator used to make the horse go forward, but they do a lot more by also acting as directional guidance. For instance, the legs may be used to keep the horse straight or on a circle, or to bend or move him sideways, such as when opening a gate. So, the legs are both accelerator and indicator.

Using your legs

To be effective, the legs should be applied close to the girth, either individually or together, when asking the horse to move forward. Used in this way, they also help to control the horse's shoulder and keep him straight. When applied further back, they help to control the hindquarters and prevent them swinging out. Bringing the outside leg back will indicate to the horse that he is expected to canter, if used in conjunction with a rein aid to the inside to tell him that this is the leg with which the rider wishes him to strike off.

Leg aids should be used actively with a nudge, tap or kick, depending on the reaction you get. It is important that once you have the reaction you want, you relax. Do not tighten or squeeze, as this tends to encourage you to tighten upwards away from your horse, creating tension rather than harmony.

Use your hands carefully

You must be gentle and considerate when using your hands, and work to co-ordinate them with your leg and seat. Resistance in the horse is caused by a lack of co-ordination between the rider's hand, seat and legs.

Little and often

Practising your exercises will ensure you achieve results, but always remember that doing a little at a time is the best way to learn. Change what you do after a few goes so that the horse does not get bored, then return to it later if you wish. Always finish on a good note.

1
This horse is overbent, with his head too low. A lighter hand and stronger leg would correct this problem.

2
This rider is pulling the reins and the horse is resisting this with a stiff jaw and tight neck. Softer responses would be achieved with a lighter 'asking' approach.

Hands
The hands may be considered as the brakes, but are actually much more than that. They balance the horse, and create a soft and subtle means of control between the rider's legs and the horse's mouth. Placing a bit in the horse's mouth creates a very sensitive area that requires understanding and sympathetic handling by the rider.

Using your hands
Simply pulling back with the reins will usually result in the horse shortening and tightening his neck muscles and becoming rather unresponsive. Where possible, use your fingers to get a reaction rather than your arm and wrist. If you need more response from the horse, flex your wrists to move the bit in his mouth. A take-and-give action is the most effective option.

Seat
Your seat can help to influence activity in the horse by your weight being lighter or heavier on his back. However, the most important aspect is to ensure that you are sitting straight, with even weight distribution, and can maintain balance whether increasing or decreasing the pace.

Do

✔ Learn to co-ordinate your leg and hand aids.

✔ Ride your horse sympathetically.

✔ Remember your horse has feelings just like you.

✔ Reward your horse with a kind word or pat.

Don't

✘ Be rough with your hands – it will hurt his mouth.

✘ Ever react in temper.

✘ Over practise any exercises – little and often is the best approach.

Coping with problems

Inevitably, there will come a time when your trainer is not around and you will have to cope on your own. While you should rarely encounter anything too serious – some everyday situations are covered on pages 80–81 – it is important to know what to do when problems occur.

In most situations, common sense will provide the answer. Ask yourself why the incident happened and decide how to cope – bearing in mind your experience, where you are and what help is to hand.

Loss of control

If control is the problem, you will need to re-establish this – for example, by slowing down as best you can through turning in a series of circles and shortening the reins until you can pull up. Remember that tugging continuously at the reins will not work: taking and giving as you circle will get a better reaction.

Play it safe

If the horse has been scared by something, talk to him, pat him and keep him on a shorter rein until you have both relaxed enough to continue as normal.

If you think that the problem could happen again, it may be better to dismount, run up the stirrups, take the reins over the horse's head and lead him home.

Learning goal

A good rider soon becomes aware of situations developing and responds and reacts to them. Tact and firmness are usually required to win any argument. Never lose your temper, however frustrating the situation.

Professional help

Sometimes your horse may develop a problem with which you must cope at the time, but in the long term you may need professional help in order to cure it.

1

Napping This occurs when you want to go one way and the horse refuses to answer your forward aids. Ask yourself if there is a genuine reason, or if he is testing you. If it is the latter, you will need to come out on top or the situation will recur. This young horse has a neckstrap around his neck for rider security and is reacting to something that has spooked him. Perseverance and firmness should win the day – losing your temper won't.

2

Rearing This can be an alarming and dangerous situation. It may be an understandable reaction to something which has genuinely frightened the horse, or a temperamental one where the horse reacts in this way with the sole purpose of frightening the rider and getting his own way.

The important thing is not to lose your balance: grab the mane or neckstrap, not the reins as this will only aggravate the situation and may pull the horse off balance and over backwards. Try turning in a circle, talking to the horse and giving him time to co-operate, then ask again tactfully.

3

Resisting The horse may resist by sticking his head up against the rider's hand aids, which may have been too strong – in which case a more subtle approach might work. He could be in pain from teeth that need attention, the rider sitting in an uncomfortable position or even the saddle pinching him. Alternatively, he may simply need riding forward more strongly in order to co-operate.

4

Head tossing This can be an uncomfortable situation and is most likely caused by discomfort, either in the mouth or from the bridle, which may be a bad fit. If the horse is young, he may be teething and therefore sore where the teeth are starting to break through the gum.

Rider fitness

Now you know what you are in for, you will have discovered how fit (or not) you are for riding. This will vary a lot from person to person, and will depend on your metabolism, your general fitness and your ability to relax when doing strenuous exercise.

Getting fit

The best way to get fit is generally to ride as much as possible and to use the riding muscles regularly, but all forms of exercise will help. You should now be finding that you can cope well with the stretches and general fitness regimes described on pages 38–39.

More emphasis on breathing will be most beneficial now you are becoming more ambitious. Any sport that is reasonably energetic will help to develop the capacity of your lungs, which will have to work harder at the faster speeds used when riding. Running, swimming, football, tennis and squash are all excellent, but cycling is probably the best of all.

Protective clothing

If you now feel really confident about riding and want to continue with it on a regular basis, it is worth investing in some breeches and boots that will protect your legs and help you to ride more comfortably. Advice from your tack store or trainer will be helpful at this stage.

Avoidance tactics

A rider's worst problem can be rubs, sores and blisters. It is well worth spending a little time working out how to avoid these – talcum powder can really come into its own! Some riders become quite badly rubbed on their legs, seat and hands.

- Wear some sort of **undergear** – such as tights or long johns – to help alleviate the friction.
- A **seat saver**, a comfortable sheepskin cover on the saddle, is a real bonus to those who suffer from seat sores. Many yards use them anyway, but if yours does not you can buy your own at your local tack store. In the meantime, a padded numnah, held in place over the saddle with a surcingle, will be the best option.
- By now, you will have discovered how tough or vulnerable your hands are. There is a huge variety of **gloves** on the market with which to make your riding experience more comfortable. Designs with rubber pimple insert on the palms have excellent grip.

Learning goal

Riding is a surprisingly physical activity, and the fitter you are, the more you will enjoy and be able to achieve. Breathing correctly throughout all exercise is one of the most important points to remember. However strenuous the activity be sure to make a conscious effort to maintain a constant breathing rate.

Protect your toes

One of the most vulnerable areas when riding or working around a horse in the stable are your toes, as these are easily trodden on. Consider buying some strong boots, or (at the very least) always wear thick socks to protect yourself in case the horse treads on your foot. You can buy boots or shoes with reinforced toecaps, which is a wise precaution. In any case, be aware and try to keep your feet out of the way of the horse's hooves.

2
Relaxing after a long ride is important. Always finish a workout with a period of walk so that the horses return from work in a relaxed and cool manner.

1
Running and cycling are excellent for developing rider fitness. Increasing your lung capacity will help you to cope with faster speeds and more energetic riding activities.

Western riding

Everyone has a picture in their mind of the traditional cowboy galloping across the plains, as seen in so many Western films. It is fast, dramatic and very spectacular – but you can start Western riding in a less ambitious way and progress to more demanding skills gradually as your confidence builds.

Seat and legs

For Western riding, the rider sits deep in the saddle with a tall, straight back and long leg. The leg is relatively ineffective in this position, but more comfortable for the style used. Rowelled spurs give the horse the lightest cue to respond – there is no need to kick.

Hands

The split reins use the minimum of contact and are generally held in one hand. The rider then 'neck reins' the horse to indicate the required direction.

Western competitions

There is a wide variety of classes for the Western rider at shows and competitions. Many can be fun for less experienced riders to start off with, before progressing to more specialized competitions. You can begin practising right away!

- **Trail riding** and **Western pleasure** provide a gentle start and plenty of opportunities for horse and rider to demonstrate their unique skills.
- **Trail riding** classes present horse and rider with some of the problems likely to be met when out on a ride.
- In **Western pleasure** classes, the horse is judged on his way of going, which must be suitable for trail riding. Judged at walk, jog (slow trot) and lope (canter), the horse must remain calm and relaxed throughout.
- Unmounted classes include **halter classes** – in which the horse is judged – and **showmanship** – in which the handler is under scrutiny.
- **Horsemanship** is an equitation class that is more for the rider. It demonstrates the rider's ability to cope with the movements required.
- Similar to horsemanship, **Western riding** requires the combination to ride to a pattern and carry out lead changes, the horse performing smoothly and obediently.
- The ranch horses have special classes, more or less reflecting their working heritage. These include **reining**, now a recognized discipline in its own right (see pages 142–143), as well as **cutting**, **working cow horse** and, of course, the spectacular **rodeo**.

1

The split reins are held in one hand – generally the left — with the back of the hand uppermost. This leaves the rider's right hand free to use the rope or lasso.

Learning goal

Start off by learning about the different gaits and how to get the horse to respond to the lightest touch. Generally the horse will move from the leg aid and you must ensure you move forward with him without letting your balance get behind from the movement of the horse. A light touch on the reins helps the slowing-up process.

2

The one-handed rider learns to neck rein her horse with a light pressure against the side of the neck, indicating to the horse that she wishes him to move in the direction away from the pressure.

3

The stirrups and stirrup leathers are designed for comfort and are very wide, incorporated into one unit called a 'fender'.

4

This rider is demonstrating the Western method of steering – using the rein against the neck to change direction.

Therapeutic riding

The use of animals as a therapy is becoming more and more widespread, as greater understanding of what can be achieved is developed. The horse is no exception and is used worldwide, both as a motivator for learning and to benefit health and well-being.

Riding is one of the few sports where it can be reliably claimed that every muscle and sense is being stimulated. As such it is a wonderfully healthy form of exercise whose benefit is slowly being accepted worldwide. Throughout history, the special bond between horse and rider has been well documented.

Learning goal

Every rider has a different perceived goal depending on their ability and the degree of their disability. If riding is found to be helpful, and it generally is, it is up to the helpers and physiotherapists to encourage each person to gain the maximum possible benefit. Outstanding performances have been demonstrated by riders at the Paralympics.

Hippotherapy

Derived from the Greek word *hippos*, meaning horse, hippotherapy is a specialized physiotherapy treatment with and on the horse, which makes use of the horse's unique movement at walk. The rhythmical, three-dimensional movement stimulates a movement in the rider's lumbar area, spine and pelvis almost identical to that produced in walking.

The horse is led, with one or two assistants helping the rider, and the rider's body responds to the movement which acts as a stimulus. This physical movement can be graded by asking the horse to produce variations in his own movement, which are used to:

• Normalize muscle tone.
• Mobilize joints.
• Stretch tight muscle groups.
• Train postural control.
• Improve balance and co-ordination.
• Strengthen muscles.

Most sessions are geared to helping children with physical disabilities, some of whom may also have associated learning and communication difficulties. Some riders may progress on to more conventional riding skills.

Specialized tack

A conventional saddle or specialized tack may be used, according to the particular difficulties of the rider. A sheepskin pad is often used to allow the rider to feel the warmth of the horse and experience his movement to the full.

Side-walkers will walk beside riders who require extra security with a leader controlling the pony.

Riding for the Disabled

The Riding for the Disabled Association is a worldwide charity, dedicated to ensuring that riders and carriage drivers receive high standards of professional tuition, tailored to their personal ambitions and capabilities.

Fully qualified instructors work closely with physio-therapists and other health officials to encourage every individual to aim for attainable goals – some modest, some very ambitious, such as competing at Paralympic level. While competition plays a healthy role, the activities focus on ensuring that both riders and those who carriage-drive derive maximum benefit from a positive and enjoyable form of therapy.

Therapeutic vaulting

Mounted gymnastics can be particularly valuable for children within the autistic spectrum, addressing many of their problems by stimulating responses. They are encouraged to watch the horse being lunged on a circle, wearing a specially equipped vaulting roller. They then learn to wait and take turns to walk or run in rhythm with the horse, and to work through exercises previously practised on a barrel or dummy. (See also pages 144–145.)

Benefits from therapeutic vaulting sessions can include:

- Developing the ability to listen and follow simple instructions.

- Building trust, interaction and communication with the horse.

- Developing co-operation.

- Improving balance and co-ordination.

Riding to music

Music is part of our everyday lives and there are numerous opportunities to use it when riding. Used as background, music can really enhance a schooling session, and for some horses it becomes as important to them as it is to us. They will perform extraordinarily well in time to music and this has been recognized in dressage competitions, so that many of the world's top contests are now decided on the ability of horse and rider to work in harmony with the music.

Back to basics

In its most basic form, music is used to add to the enjoyment of gymkhana games: musical sacks and its variations (see pages 96–97 and 140–141) have long been a favourite with children. Blowing a whistle would be an easy alternative, but there is no doubt that the music adds to the fun and excitement of the occasion.

Dressage to music

If you would like to try riding some dressage movements to music, first consider the type of music required to fit the various paces.

Do not be too ambitious to start with. Work out a simple but interesting programme showing the movements required in walk, trot and canter, so that your music does not sound too variable.

Once you have found some music that is suitable for each pace and inspires the trot or canter, you then need to check that it is right for your horse. A powerful horse with very definite rhythm will be best suited to powerful music; a more delicate mover will be better suited to a lighter tune that will not overpower the horse's natural way of going.

When you have decided on suitable music (which you should also enjoy riding to), you will then need to time your programme and work out the duration of the walk, trot and canter within it, so that you can compile your music appropriately on tape. You will then be set to perform your masterpiece in a dressage-to-music competition!

It is always a good idea to get the help of a knowledgeable friend who can cast a critical eye over your programme. A little word of advice can turn a dull performance into a star attraction. Go and watch the experts in a live show to get some ideas before you start. There are also training videos on the art of riding to music. It won't be long before you feel confident to show off to your friends your new found skill.

Using a metronome
A metronome can be very useful in determining your horse's natural rhythm and finding music that will fit with it.

1

It is important that the music suits the horse and emphasizes the pace at which the horse is moving. Music for the trot, as demonstrated here, would need to be in a 2-beat rhythm.

2

When practising a special theme it is very important for everyone to keep up together and work with the music once your programme has been decided. Each team member must be aware of when to catch up or slow down to the music.

Getting the beat

Remember that a horse's trot is two-time and the canter three-time (see pages 58–59 and 90–91), so it is worth thinking about using a stirring march for your horse's trot and something like a waltz for the canter work.

Teamwork

Some riding clubs organize quadrilles to music to be ridden by four or more people together. They are fun to set up and a great way of learning to ride together as a team.

Competitions for such teams are very hotly contested, with an enormous amount of work and months of practice involved in organizing music, ridden content and costumes to blend together successfully.

LEARNING TO JUMP

It is most riders' dream one day to ride over fences and experience that wonderful feeling of flying through the air as your horse takes off. Jumping is an exhilarating feeling, but it will take a little longer than a weekend to be ready to take on this particular challenge. Nevertheless, aspirations are what life is all about, and the aim of this chapter is to set you on your way to achieving this as soon as you feel confident enough in your riding.

How the horse jumps

The horse is a natural jumper: the ability to leap over streams and logs is essential when escaping from predators. The jump is really an extension of the canter, in which the explosion of power goes upwards over the obstacle rather than forwards into the next canter stride.

Learning goal

The balance and position of the rider over the fence is the secret of success. The rider must ensure that his body remains in balance to ensure the horse is unhindered as progress is made and jumps become larger as the horse is airborne for that little bit longer.

1

Approach The horse is lowering his head to prepare for take-off. The rider allows freedom and goes forward.

2

Take-off The horse's hindlegs come underneath him as he propels himself into the air. The rider follows with her body and hands.

Stages of the jump
The jump has five distinct stages:

Approach The horse measures the fence and prepares himself to jump by lowering his head.

Take-off The horse propels himself upwards, pushing from his hindlegs and lifting the forelegs.

Flight The momentum created by the take-off carries the horse through the air and over the fence in an arc.

Landing The forelegs stretch downwards to land and the horse's head starts to come up as the hindlegs touch the ground.

Move-off As the horse rebalances himself from the landing, his forelegs come up again as he strides away from the fence.

3

Flight The horse is airborne over the fence. The rider maintains a balanced position with enough freedom allowed to the horse's head and neck.

4

Landing The horse lands on first one foreleg and then a split second later on the other, while the head comes up to help balance him as the hindlegs descend. The rider's weight comes back at this stage, so that the horse can take the next stride unhindered.

Suitability and training

Before the rider starts to learn to jump, the horse will have gone through a gradual training process to prepare him mentally and physically for the demands jumping places on him. Most horses love to jump and are generally fairly athletic, but (like us) they are not all cut out for it and some are naturally better than others.

It is important that the horse has been given a consistent build-up over fences. A typical training progression might be:

1 Small, single fences.
2 Larger single fences.
3 Line or grid of fences.
4 Line or grid of fences incorporating different striding patterns.
5 Course of jumps, gradually increasing in size and complexity over time.

Influential factors
There are various factors that influence how the horse jumps – these may either help or hinder him:

- The pace coming into the fence must be forward and balanced, whether in trot or canter.
- The size of the fence must be suitable for both horse and rider, taking into account their ability and current level of competence.
- The take-off and landing surfaces must be safe and consistent.

The approach

The canter is the most important pace when jumping and is crucial to the quality of the jump. Unfortunately, riders often tend to interfere with the horse's stride on the approach – this upsets his balance and often creates problems that would not otherwise occur.

Learning goal
If you can master a balanced, forward and consistent stride into the fence, the rest will be easy.

Achieving rhythm and balance
The canter must have the two vital ingredients of forward rhythm and balance, which cannot work without each other. To balance your horse, you need to keep his head up by raising your hands and encourage his hindlegs to come up with more energy underneath him by stronger use of your hands, so that he can support his own weight more effectively. This enables him to lighten his shoulders, so that his strides are bouncier and free. In this way, the horse will find it easy to jump the fence.

If the horse is allowed to put his head down, his weight and balance will be too far forward on his forehand and he will not be able to jump so well, or will produce a 'flat' jump.

Seeing a stride
Always wait for the fence to 'come to you' – do not try to 'see a stride' in order to get the horse to take off in the correct place. Striding will never be consistent if you increase pace or slow down. Just practise a forward, consistent, balanced canter into each fence – then where you are becomes irrelevant.

Developing style
Style is very important and as a beginner you may find it difficult at first not to get left behind over a fence, while you are still getting used to the feel of jumping.

- You will need to ride a couple of stirrup holes shorter, as you will rise a little out of the saddle over the jump.
- Practise cantering with your seat out of the saddle and your weight forward, with your legs remaining on the horse's sides consistently.
- Your arms should follow a line from the elbow, through the forearm and wrist, to the bit. Try to keep a soft but consistent feel on the reins.

It will take practice to be able to co-ordinate all this together.

Motivating your horse
How easy all this is depends very much on the horse's natural way of going. It is easier to maintain rhythm and balance on a naturally forward horse than on a lazy one, so with a horse of this temperament you will need to motivate him somehow – possibly with a sharp, fast canter before attempting to jump.

1

The horse has got a little close to this cross-pole, and so to be able to clear it he has made a very rounded, athletic jump. This will throw the rider backwards on landing. Note how she has pushed her arms forward in an effort not to interfere with the horse's mouth.

2

In this picture, the horse has taken off too early and is already on the descent over the fence. Luckily, the rider has done all she can to give the horse freedom to sort himself out as best he can and balance is being restored. Pulling backwards on the reins would have spelt total disaster!

Secret of success

For a successful jump it is vital that you can keep the forward rhythm and balance all the way to the fence.

Problems

Difficulties will inevitably arise from time to time, but do not worry about them too much at this stage. Think about what happened, then go back and try again. Ask yourself:

• Am I in balance?

• Am I being left behind?

• Am I too far forward?

These are the crucial questions and the answers are likely to influence whether the horse takes off too early, too late – or not at all! (See also pages 132–133.)

Correct position

Once you have really mastered the canter and can successfully steer the horse over poles on the ground, the next step is to jump over small fences. Practise cantering around the arena with your seat out of the saddle and your weight down into the balls of your feet. Steer around the jumps and get your horse going forward and balanced, as described on pages 126–127.

Your first jump

Your trainer will put up a few small jumps around the school and perhaps a pole or two on the ground. A cross-pole is an ideal starter fence, as it encourages you to jump in the middle. Approach the fence straight in trot to start with and jump it a couple of times before trying in canter.

Maintain an even canter and allow the fence to 'come to you', rather than increasing speed towards the jump. Ride the fence two or three times, then try another. Remember to shift your weight forward over the fence and allow your hands to slide forward up the neck as you get more confident and become less tight in your arms. Your horse will need all the freedom he can to jump cleanly.

Secrets of success
- Look up and between the horse's ears on the approach.
- Keep your weight into your heels and your legs on the horse.
- Maintain balance with the horse throughout the jump.
- Do not get in front of the horse's movement on take-off, or get left behind over the fence.
- Allow your hands to follow the rein towards the horse's mouth during the jump.

1
The horse is just about to land and the rider is starting to sit up in the saddle reaching for the next stride.

Learning goal
If you can, watch more experienced riders at a show and study how they ride. It should look effortless – it is those riders who seem to flow with their horses that you need to emulate.

2

This rider has allowed the horse to make a lovely athletic jump over the fence with her weight balanced on the horse's withers. She is allowing her hand to give enough freedom to the horse's head as he jumps.

Practice makes perfect

Do not overdo your early jumping lessons, as muscles that are unused to the exertion may complain. You can, however, pop over several fences if all is going well and your horse remains calm and relaxed.

- Practise turning into fences and getting a good, straight approach.
- Ride away from each fence in a straight line.
- Do not allow the horse to jump and then race back towards his friends – it can be quite unseating if he makes a quick turn while you are still regaining your balance following a jump.

Once you feel confident over small fences, increase the size very gradually and add a back pole to make a small parallel.

Take care
Be careful never to overface yourself or your horse. Confidence is everything, so do not take risks – it takes time to build it up and one rash moment can undermine all your hard work for months.

Types of jump

- Single fences are called verticals or uprights.

- Two poles one behind the other are called a parallel or spread.

- Two fences with one, two or three strides in-between are called a double.

- Three fences with one, two or three strides in-between are called a treble.

Grids and cross-country fences

Grids are used to encourage the horse to be more athletic and to help him to balance himself over a series of jumps and poles. They are very useful in helping you to react quickly, and to balance and think about what the horse is doing as you jump the obstacles.

First grids

Grids should start as a simple exercise and then be built up gradually to achieve what is required. By shortening or lengthening the strides between the different elements, the horse can be helped to balance himself better and make a better shape over the fence. A pole on the ground, followed by a cross-pole, then another pole on the ground,

followed by a vertical, makes a good starting point. The striding must be adjusted to suit your horse, but is generally around 3 m (10 ft) per element. As you negotiate each obstacle, you must sit up and balance yourself over the poles and allow your upper body to move forward over the jumps.

Bounces – jumps with no non-jumping strides – and parallels can also be incorporated into grids. These will help the horse to shorten and lengthen over the different elements. However, be careful not to confuse the horse by overdoing the complexity of the grid. Two or three jumps is enough, as a grid is quite demanding, both physically and mentally.

Making a start over a simple cross-country fence. The rider is looking down instead of up and forwards. Her leathers are too long, but her leg is on her horse directing him.

1

Grids require a greater degree of balance and control than single fences, as you have to negotiate poles and fences. Sit up over the poles and keep your weight forward over the fences.

2

The rider is beginning to sit up on landing, ready to ride over the pole on the ground.

Cross-country fences

Once you feel confident in the arena, jumping cross-country fences is a natural progression. Starting with simple fences, such as logs on the ground, you can progress to other small fences such as straw bales, small ditches and hedges, post-and-rails, and then fences going up and down slopes.

Cross-country riding is all about balanced speed over fences – it should not be done flat out but in a consistent, faster rhythm than over show-jumps. Because of the faster pace, you will need to shorten your stirrup leathers and ride with a strong leg, while sitting forward and in balance with your horse.

Riding technique

You should sit up and hold your horse together as he jumps the different fences. Ride onwards at wider fences such as parallels, and sit up and maintain forward impulsion at single or combination fences. Your trainer will advise you on how to approach the more specialized fences.

Learning goal

Riding at speed over cross-country fences requires a direct responsibility for control. It is essential that you feel able to stop or slow down when necessary so you will need to practise this.

Equipment for cross-country riding

Control is very important and it may be necessary to adjust your 'brakes' by using a different bit for cross-country riding. A running martingale to help with turning – it helps to control the degree of the bend – and a more effective noseband can both make a big difference (see pages 44–45 and 106–107).

Protect your horse's legs with suitable boots, and use overreach boots ('bell boots') to prevent him catching his heels or bruising himself if he accidentally hits a fence.

Make sure you are wearing an effective skullcap and back protector for jumping.

3
Here they are negotiating the pole and preparing to jump the fence at the next part of the grid.

4
The take-off shows the horse lifting off the ground in front, but the two front legs are not quite together.

Coping with problems

Just occasionally, however hard you try, things do not go quite right! It is best to be prepared and know what to do in such situations. Then work out why things happened as they did and how you are going to put them right.

Poor approach

Most problems in riding arise because the rider has failed to prepare adequately, so that the horse does not get sufficient warning of what he is expected to do. With jumping, this usually means that the approach has not been straight, so the horse has not had enough time to assess the fence he is supposed to be jumping. There may also not have been sufficient speed for the horse to jump the fence with ease, or the fence may have been unsuitable or too big for the experience and ability of that horse-and-rider combination.

Solution: In most cases, a second attempt at riding towards the fence straight and with sufficient impulsion will solve the problem.

Behind or in front of the movement

Sometimes the rider gets too far forward and is in front of the horse's movement, making it difficult for him to lift his forehand. In this situation, the horse will eventually become demoralized. Sit up and drive him onwards positively.

The opposite can also happen – the rider sits too far back. Then, on take-off she catches the horse in the mouth and on landing crashes down on his back. He may forgive this once, but probably not twice!

Solution: If you have either of these problems, you need to improve your balance and technique before attempting to jump again.

Rider nerves

There are occasions when the rider comes towards the fence with good intentions, but as it gets nearer she communicates panic to the horse, who obligingly stops. Do not worry if this happens to you – everyone experiences this at some stage in their career.

Solution: If this has happened to you, it may be an indication that you are not yet quite as ready to be brave as you thought. Or, if you are, you may just need someone to tell you to get on with it!

Learning goal

Do not become demoralized when things go wrong. At some stage, they are bound to go better or worse than they did the last time. Just stop and think about why a problem occurred and then set out to put it right with even more determination than before.

Safety first

Use a back protector in case of unlucky tumbles and ensure that your hat is securely fastened, you are wearing gloves and, if necessary, carrying a whip. Always check the girth before jumping.

1

There is always a drop into a water jump, but sitting up well as you enter the water will help to avoid the above.

2

This young rider was obviously keener than her pony. Most children tend to cut corners on their approach to a fence: you must ride straight, ride forward and sit up well to be effective at a fence.

3

A run-out is usually caused by the rider's reins being too long, giving the horse a perfect opportunity to do his own thing. Fences sited along a hedge line require strong riding if the horse is not to use this as an excuse to shy inwards.

GOING FORWARDS

This chapter gives a brief overview of the many and varied equestrian activities available to you, now that you have mastered the basics of riding and jumping. There is so much on offer, whether you wish to remain a leisure rider, become more of a competitor, or even want to make a career out of horses. The most popular equestrian sports are all covered here, but there are plenty of other opportunities available through equestrian clubs, including polo, handball, le trec, driving, team chasing and racing, to name just a few.

Further opportunities

Now that you have started riding and discovered what fun it all is, met new friends and perhaps worked out which aspects you really enjoy, the time will come when you want to get to know more about your chosen sport.

There is a huge number of different opportunities available within the equestrian scene and it is well worth finding out a bit more about all of these before deciding which is the one for you. Some people enjoy a varied, all-round approach; others like to specialize in one aspect. Whatever you decide, it is well worth mastering the basics of one before embarking on another.

1

Polo is a very popular sport played by opposing teams of four a side. It is a fast and exciting game requiring a good eye and natural balance.

2

For those with disabilites, it is often possible to ride in a local disabled riding group. It provides a wonderful therapy for many conditions and is a great boost for confidence.

Magazines
The numerous horsey magazines available are a great source of information and advertisements to help you find out more about the various equestrian sports.

Riding schools and clubs
Joining a local riding school or club can be one way of learning about the opportunities available. Some are very proactive, others less so, but all should be able to give helpful advice to point you in the right direction.

Shows and events
The larger horse shows often include trade stands where you can browse and collect information between classes. Shows are also an opportunity to talk to people already involved in various sports and receive advice.

3
Team chasing is fast, fun and a popular pastime in the UK and elsewhere. Teams of three or four ride a set cross-country course, usually to a preset time.

Breed specialists

There is also the opportunity to become involved with a specific breed or type of horse or pony. The native breeds of Britain, or the specialized breeds from the USA, Spain and other countries, all have their own particular attributes. There are also particular types, such as the cob or sport horse, and other horses defined by their coat colour, such as the palomino or coloured horse. All these and dozens more have special classes or activities related to what they can do or were bred for.

A career with horses
You may be considering a career with horses. You might want to become a groom, an instructor or a competitor, or help voluntarily with the local Pony Club, riding club or disabled riding or therapy group. Whatever your choice, you can be assured of a warm welcome. Horse people are fun and friendly and have that mutual interest in the horse, which dominates their lives in so many very different ways.

The World Wide Web
You can surf the Internet to find out more about the different equestrian sports available both in your home country and around the world.

Riding holidays

Holidays are a great way not only to meet new, like-minded friends, but also to increase your riding ability in a relaxed atmosphere. There are literally hundreds of different activities available and so much to choose from, but do be sure you find out exactly what is involved and what you are letting yourself in for before booking.

Types of holiday

You name it, and you can do it. Choose from:

- Riding safaris.
- American dude ranch holidays, where you can experience ranch life at first hand.
- Instructional riding holidays.
- Family riding holidays, including some trekking holidays.

1

Splashing through water in spectacular scenery is a great form of relaxation and many riding holidays include a bit of riding in water or along rivers.

2

Seaside holidays are always popular but care must be taken to ensure that those in charge are aware of incoming tides and where and when it is safe to ride.

Trek-style holidays

Throughout the world, there are amazing treks available through stunning countryside, from Andalucia to Iceland, and the Himalayas to South America. Every country has its own unique features and seeing them on horseback is an equally unique experience.

Holidays can range from a basic camping-type vacation to more comfortable treks, which might include staying in farmsteads or hotels.

Preparation

Before setting off on a riding holiday:

- Make sure you have sensible clothes, your safety hat, gloves and suitable boots or shoes.
- Check your own or the holiday organizer's insurance.
- Read all the information provided by the organizer to ensure you know what is required and what is and is not provided.
- Ring up to clarify any points you are unsure about – it is too late once you arrive!

Riding expertise

Inevitably, riding standards on holiday trips vary enormously. Most travel companies have adopted a semi-standardized code of expertise, and ask their clients to indicate in which category they think they belong. Unfortunately, perception and reality do not always agree, but nevertheless this helps to provide more exact information about riding capabilities and allows organizers to provide suitable horses for their clients.

Beginner Never ridden, or very limited experience and cannot yet rise to the trot.

Intermediate Reasonably confident in all paces and has had a few lessons.

Competent Rides regularly, fit, and confident riding and jumping outdoors. A competent rider may have her own horse.

Experienced Very fit and confident, capable of riding and jumping most horses in all paces.

3

Wherever your riding holiday is taking place, it is important to know what to expect and to be prepared for changeable weather.

Mounted games

Many riders started their careers doing some sort of mounted games, usually through the Pony Club (see pages 96–97). Although some games reflect the local traditions or customs, many similar ones are practised worldwide.

Learn as you play

Mounted games are enjoyable, exciting, varied and a great way to build friendships. They are mainly for children or teenagers, although some adults do participate, and it is here that the pony really excels. Without realizing it, you will be learning important lessons in balance, control, impulsion and co-ordination, as well as it all being great fun.

Pony qualities

The mounted-games pony must be:

- Quick and alert.
- Agile and supple.
- Obedient.
- Able to remain in good balance and rhythm throughout.

The right pony

A good pony is essential for mounted games and they come in all shapes and sizes. You do not need a smart pony to be successful, but you do need one that is well schooled to respond to the demands placed upon him and quick but calm in the heat of the games played.

Training

The training of the pony is vital and it is worth starting immediately you decide to participate.

- It is essential that the pony is responsive to the aids: he must be able to go from walk straight into canter and come to a halt quickly.
- He must also be taught to respond to neck reining, as many of the games must be ridden one-handed so that you can use the other hand to pick up or drop objects at various points.
- The pony must also lead well, as you may have to lead him to another part of the arena as part of one of the races.
- He must be quite used to coloured buckets, flags, bottles and other unusual objects, and to seeing his rider in a sack or wiggling through tyres!

You can accentuate your aids with verbal commands, so teaching your pony words such as 'Go' and 'Stop' will help.

1

The ever-popular bending race (see pages 96–97) requires great balance, skill and co-ordination. It is important to go a little wider around the last pole so that you can make a complete turn for the way back.

2
Precision games like this bucket-stepping race take practice to perfect. The pony must remain calm and not pull at the rider while being led.

3
Another type of precision game, which involves picking up individual mugs from on top of a bucket. Races like this demand balance, co-ordination and perseverance.

4
Vaulting onto or off your pony is an essential skill if you are involved in mounted games where speed is crucial.

Rider skills

Your own skills must be many and varied. For example, the sack race requires a certain level of competence in running and hopping!

Being able to vault on and off is a vital part of the picture, so practise this in an enclosed arena until you feel competent.

Types of game
Most mounted games fall into one of two categories:

1 Games of speed. These generally consist of pony and rider getting from one point to another in the fastest time.
2 Games of precision. These games involve picking up items and replacing them somewhere else as quickly as possible.

Reining

Of all the Western classes – and there are many (see pages 116–117) – reining is one of the most popular. It even had the honour of being shown as a demonstration sport at the Sydney Olympics in 2000.

Development of reining

The sport of reining originates from movements used with ranch horses when working cattle. The reining horse is required to move in a less collected and freer manner than some types of show horse, but it does perform to a certain extent as a Western dressage horse, demonstrating many of the movements required of it on the ranch adapted to competitive use.

Reining requirements

To be successful in reining contests, the horse must demonstrate extreme obedience to almost imperceptible cues, exerted more by the movement of the rider's weight than anything else. To become fully trained, a reining horse will undergo a slow and patient schooling programme before he is able to perform the movements required of him. These include:

• Specific patterns at the lope and gallop.
• Flying lead changes.
• Roll-backs (180-degree pivots on the hindlegs).
• Spins (through 360 degrees, at breakneck speed).

1

Horse and rider perform patterns and circles at the lope and gallop. The horse must be extremely responsive and obedient to the subtlest cue from his rider.

2
Spins consist of rapid 360-degree turns and are often breathtaking to watch.

3
The most spectacular of all reining movements is the sliding stop. The horse literally slides from gallop to halt by shifting his weight so far back on to his haunches that he slides to a halt in a crouched position. Special shoes called 'sliding plates' are used to accentuate this movement.

Western 'dressage'
Reining is sometimes also called Western dressage, which gives a good clue as to what the discipline is all about.

Reining manoeuvres

The set patterns laid out for reining horses involve various manoeuvres, including:

Walk-ins Demonstrating a relaxed start.

Stops Slowing from a lope to a stop.

Spins A series of 360-degree turns on the one spot.

Roll-backs A 180-degree reversal of forward motion towards the opposite direction.

Backup An extended rein-back over at least 10 feet (3 metres).

Hesitate The ability to stand relaxed at a set time within a pattern.

Lead changes Flying changes as specified within the pattern.

Run-downs Runs to demonstrate control and increase in speed to the stop.

Vaulting

Vaulting can best be described as gymnastics on horseback. As with so many equestrian disciplines, it started off as a method of improving skills among cavalry officers and has now developed into an international sport. Performed on a cantering horse, it is practised in over 30 countries, mainly by teenagers, both competitively and recreationally.

Development of vaulting

Vaulting has, of course, been performed in one form or another since humans first leapt on to a horse in early efforts to tame him. It has undergone a variety of changes since then, including being used by the military, in circuses and as trick-riding displays. Today, vaulting includes three disciplines:

- Team classes (consisting of eight vaulters and one reserve).
- Individual classes.
- Pas de deux (two horses and two riders).

Vaulting classes

Team vaulters must be 18 years or under, but the individual classes have no age limit. Each class has two sections – compulsory exercises and a freestyle programme – both performed on a cantering horse moving anticlockwise. The judges are positioned around the arena so that they can see from all angles. The skill, balance and co-ordination required at top level is breathtaking, where the vaulters' colours add to the spectacle. To join a vaulting group, contact your equestrian society for information on where to get started.

Vaulting advantages

There is no doubt that those who have benefited from vaulting at a young age have a natural seat on a horse, which stands them in good stead for the rest of their riding careers.

Vaulting to the top

As one of the International Equestrian Federation's (FEI) seven main sports, vaulting has a world championship that takes place every four years. It was included as a demonstration sport at the Los Angeles Olympics in 1984.

1

The vaulting team is a very special unit in which everyone must work together. Vaulting is sometimes used therapeutically where the continuous movement of the horse helps to improve the rider's agility and co-ordination.

2

The elegance and expertise required for vaulting is well demonstrated here. The horse must be consistent, smooth in his canter and well trained on the lunge.

The vaulting team

The team required for competition includes:

Vaulters They must be dependable as they need to rely on each other.

Horse A very special animal, that is strong enough to cope with up to three vaulters on top at any one time. He must be steady, well balanced, and able to maintain a rhythm for eight minutes in the compulsory section and five minutes in the freestyle.

Lunger This team member controls the horse and the rhythm throughout the programme, and is key to the whole performance.

Trainer This may be the same person as the lunger, or someone who oversees the performance watching from the edge to ensure that the team gels as a high-performance unit.

Endurance riding

Endurance riding is an increasingly popular sport that is designed to test the speed and stamina of the horse, combined with the riding ability of the rider. Ridden over various distances and often in some wild but stunning countryside, rides take place with the purpose of competing within a set time or achieving the fastest time, both being subject to having a sound horse in good condition who has passed the various vet checks along the route.

1

Endurance riding can take you to different countries and over many different types of terrain. In Dubai, endurance riding is hugely popular and the Arab is one of the most successful breeds used for the sport.

Types of ride

There are two basic categories of endurance rides. The lower-distance rides are designed as gentle introductions to the sport for novice horses and riders. These include competitive trail rides of between 30 and 80 km (20 and 50 miles) and have set upper and lower speed limits.

Placings are given based on a combination of speed and heartrate recovery time, or awards are given to all those achieving a certain standard. At the top levels on rides above 80 km (50 miles)

up to the championship distances of 160 km (100 miles) in one day, placings are awarded on the basis of first-past-the-post and the vet's inspection. Any horse failing the veterinary judging is automatically disqualified from the competition, even if he has finished the ride. The welfare of the horse is paramount, despite the demands placed on him at the top levels. Endurance riding is a sport where horsemanship and understanding of the horse's state of fitness plays a vital part.

2

Clothing and tack needs to be comfortable, as the slightest rub can become serious over long distances. These three look fit and happy riding along the edge of the sea, but sand getting up under leg boots could cause irritation.

3

The vet checks are the time when back-up crew come into their own, watering the horse, cooling him and preparing him for the next stage. The rider will also need refreshment and support.

Choosing a horse

The ideal endurance horse stands around 152–163 cm (15–16 hands high), with good, athletic conformation and excellent feet. He must be willing and able, but also requires a laid-back temperament to enable him to remain relaxed at all times.

Getting started

It takes several months to build up the fitness necessary in both horse and rider to compete at the longer events and to learn how to ride effectively, so that you conserve your horse's energy. Starting in trail rides and working your way up is the best way to learn and build up the experience and knowledge required to know how, why and when to go slowly or to push on to win.

Back-up crew

The back-up crew, who look after you and your horse, are vital to success and usually consist of family and friends. The crew follow you throughout the ride, meeting up with you to prepare the horse for the veterinary inspections that take place along the route. This involves:

• Cooling down the horse.

• Giving him the correct amount of water to drink.

• Washing him down to lower his temperature and make him comfortable by removing sweat and dirt.

• Checking for any injuries.

• Monitoring the heartrate.

• Checking that shoes are in good order.

Once the horse passes the inspection, the crew prepare him for the next stage. Theirs is as busy a day as the rider's, but the job is both fun and interesting.

Equitation classes

Many countries – including the USA, Canada, Australia, New Zealand and South Africa – take the skill of the rider very seriously and have devised classes that are designed to test this. These have certainly helped to raise the standards coming through the grades to top levels in jumping and other classes.

Format

Before entering an equitation class, scrutinize the rules in detail and try to watch a few classes in advance so that you know what to expect. The standards are generally divided into novice, intermediate and open classes, and may also be age-related. The classes themselves may be divided into three phases.

Rewards for excellence

While each national federation has designed their own format, the principles are much the same. The judges are looking for effective riding that will help riders as they progress into whatever type of riding they finally choose. The rider's position is therefore scrutinized carefully, and the ability to create rhythm and balance so that movements are performed neatly and in an unhurried, even pace, is rewarded.

Phase 1

This is a set test of movements designed to test riding ability. These may include such skills as riding a figure-of-eight, riding without stirrups, guiding the horse with only one hand on the reins, and so on.

Phase 2

This phase is generally more difficult, and only a certain percentage of the top scores may be asked to complete it. There may be a jump or two, and exercises to test the rider's skill and balance over them can include landing on the correct lead, jumping on a circular track and changes of rein over the fences. They may also be required to do small circles, serpentines or even shoulder in or perform pirouettes.

Phase 3

The third phase is generally over a course of jumps, where the rhythm, balance and flow are all taken into account, along with the rider's position and performance as a whole. The judges may hold up cards to give the scores in this phase, or sometimes in phase two as well.

Added extras

In some countries, equitation competitions are performed side-saddle or in costume, adding to their appeal and entertainment value.

Riding skills

Equitation classes are specially designed to test the rider's skill in a variety of different ways. In countries where these classes are widely practised, it is noticeable how many more riders are able to demonstrate basic riding skills. All riders should, after a period of time, be able to demonstrate the most simple skilled movements, such as riding with one hand and opening gates whilst mounted.

1
This rider is demonstrating an extended canter during a workout for the judges. The position is good and the horse is looking happy and confident.

2
This rider, performing in a costume side-saddle equitation class, is in a good position over the fence and nicely balanced so that she does not interfere in any way with the horse's jump. With the weight generally further back than on a normal saddle, it is important for the rider to give adequate freedom of rein to the horse.

Showing

Showing is one of the most hotly contested equestrian activities and also one of the most varied. It is the horse that is being judged, generally on its type or breed, so correct conformation is crucial to success. In some classes, the horse must be presented in an acceptable way for that particular section or class.

1

This impressive line-up of show hacks in the UK demonstrates the work that goes into the presentation. Beautifully plaited (braided) manes, coloured browbands and double bridles are accepted presentation for this type of class.

Secret of success

Watch the professionals and learn from them. They know how to impress but all of them started out like you, as an amateur, and reached the top through hard work and learning from others.

Types of class

Classes are held for horses and ponies presented in-hand (led by the handler), with special emphasis on youngstock, mares and foals, and stallions. There are also ridden classes divided into height or age categories. Different classes cater for every conceivable type of animal and what they are used for today.

Showing in-hand

In-hand classes generally require the horse to be shown in a bridle unless he is under two years old. He will be required to stand and be led up in walk and trot in front of the judge. If you intend to participate, find out from friends or from the society that makes the rules exactly what is involved, and prepare accordingly.

Youngsters need time to learn how to show themselves, so it is a good idea to practise running up in-hand with them. The horse should move straight, with you leading from the near side. Carry a show cane and wear suitable shoes for running. Some classes recommend suitable clothing for the handler – such as hacking jacket, collar and tie, trousers and a hat – while others do not specify. Above all, you need to look neat, tidy and discreet: it is the horse the judge should be looking at, not you!

2

A panoramic view of hunter judging in the USA, as the horse performs over a course of natural fences in this large arena. Hunters may be required to work on the flat or over fences.

3

The child's pony is always a favourite, as these spectacular little animals perform for their young jockeys. This one, with his rider bedecked in rosettes, has caught the photographer's eye.

Ridden showing

There are a huge variety of ridden classes, from pony classes and breed classes to classes for hunters, hacks and cobs. There is something for everyone, but you may need guidance as to what you should enter.

In some classes, you are required to give a brief individual show. This is your personal moment to catch the judge's eye. You must be quick, slick and impressive, as you will only have about one-and-a-half minutes in which to perform.

In some classes the judge will ride the horses as part of the test, to assess how well schooled and comfortable they are. Make sure your saddlery is suitable and that your stirrups and leathers are the right length for the judge. If you don't win a prize the first time, don't despair – learn what is required and, in time, the rewards will come.

Rules and regulations

Each show will run its classes according to the rules laid down by the relevant governing bodies of that particular section or breed. Larger shows may require exhibitors to be members of the relevant show societies in order to compete.

Dressage, eventing and showjumping

The three Olympic sports of dressage, eventing and showjumping are the best-known of all equestrian activities and are practised worldwide. At the top level, the magical movements performed by the dressage horse, the boldness and bravery exhibited over cross-country fences by the eventer, and the size and precision of the jumps taken by the showjumper are awe-inspiring to behold. Yet there are plenty of opportunities for less experienced riders to get involved.

Dressage

Pure dressage consists of the horse performing set movements in a small or large arena (see pages 78–79). Tests are tailored to suit the different standards and each movement is marked out of ten. Each national federation sets their own tests and rules around those of the International Equestrian Federation (FEI), which governs the discipline worldwide and arranges the international calendar.

1

Dressage is a test of training and harmony between horse and rider. This rider has the horse well balanced as they work through the set test. In eventing, dressage is the first of the three phases.

Training

'Dressage' essentially means training and is all about performing movements in all paces correctly and in harmony. The horse needs correct schooling over a period of time, to develop the muscles and balance that will enable him to perform progressively up through the grades. The rider needs to understand the principles and work with a trainer to achieve those goals.

Eventing

Eventing is like an equestrian triathlon in that it combines three disciplines into one. The first phase consists of a dressage test suitable for the standard set for the competition. This is usually followed by one round of show-jumps. The final phase is the cross-country, when horse and rider tackle a course of solid fences that may include ditches, banks, water and single, double or multiple combination obstacles, all to be ridden within an optimum time. This format takes place over one, two or three days, and horses and riders progress up through the grades.

International additions
At international three-day events the cross-country phase includes an endurance element of roads and tracks, plus a steeplechase course tackled at the gallop.

2

Cross-country riding is exciting and really tests the skill and bravery of horse and rider. It is the most influential of the three phases in eventing and requires plenty of practice before competing.

3

This young rider has started to learn about showjumping at a young age. Concentration and a will to win are essential to be successful in this competitive sport. In eventing, the showjumping phase is usually the last, but in some events it takes place before the cross-country.

Showjumping

In this sport, horse and rider tackle a course of brightly coloured jumps, which includes a variety of fences and striding challenges. Depending on the standard of class and its rules, a jump-off between the clear rounds then takes place to determine the winner. This is over a raised but shortened course and is sometimes timed; if not, a second jump-off may take place, again over a raised course.

Testing horse and rider
Different competitions are designed to test riders in different ways, and as the standard of classes rises so do the demands on height, speed and athletic ability. Use of the arena, accuracy over the fences and the training of the horse and rider are all tested by the course designer.

Making further progress

World Champion Rodrigo Pessoa. His dedication and attention to detail earned him the coveted world title at an early age – helped, no doubt, by his legendary father Nelson, who inspired a generation with his quiet but very effective professionalism.

Whatever you now decide to do with your riding, I hope you will have acquired a thorough insight into what the sport is all about and how to set out to achieve your aims. Hopefully, you will also have experienced the sheer enjoyment of riding a horse.

The opportunities are endless, and for those with ambitions to progress there is a whole new world out there to help you realize these, if that is where you want to go. The horse world is friendly and fun, and there is always someone who knows someone who would be happy to point you in the right direction. Good luck!

Glossary

Action How a horse moves. It is important that the horse moves straight if he is to remain sound.

Aged Horse over eight years old.

Aids Signals a rider uses to communicate with the horse. Natural aids are the hands, seat, legs and voice. Artificial aids include whips, spurs and martingales.

Bars (1) Parts of the gums at the side of the horse's mouth where there are no teeth and where the bit lies. (2) Metal hooks or bars that are part of the saddle tree and from which the stirrup leathers hang.

Bit Part of the bridle, usually made from metal, which lies in the horse's mouth to give the rider control and to which the reins are attached.

Bone Measurement around a horse's leg taken just below the knee. The larger the circumference, the greater the weight the horse can carry.

Breaking in The process of training the horse to accept a rider on his back. Sometimes called 'backing', this is done by experienced trainers and should not be attempted by beginners.

Breastplate Neckstrap that fastens to the front of the saddle and also runs between the forelegs to the girth. It prevents the saddle slipping backwards, especially when galloping. A breastgirth has a similar effect.

Bridle Combination of straps that fits around a horse's head and to which the bit and reins are attached.

Brood mare Mare kept just for breeding, often after finishing her riding career.

Brushing Bad action, where the lower legs move so closely that they strike into each other, causing injury.

Cast When a horse lies down and is unable to get up.

Chaff Straw, or a mixture of hay and straw, chopped into short lengths and added to the feed to provide more fibre.

Clear round Completing a course of jumps without any penalties.

Clip (1) Shearing off the winter coat to prevent a horse sweating too much when worked. (2) Part of a horseshoe that turns over the edge of the hoof to help keep the shoe in place.

Colic Stomach ache in the horse, often caused by bad feeding or too much water being drunk while the horse is still hot after exercise.

Colt Uncastrated male horse under three years of age.

Conformation Shape of the horse's body, the way it is put together.

Crupper Broad strap that is fixed to the back of the saddle and runs around the horse's tail, to prevent the saddle from slipping too far forward. Often necessary with small, fat ponies.

Dam Mother of a foal.

Dished face Term used to describe a face with concave profile, as in an Arab horse.

Dishing Poor action, where the horse's front feet are thrown out to the sides.

Double bridle Bridle with two bits, used on highly trained horses for dressage and showing.

Dressage Elegant equestrian sport in which horses are trained to be very obedient to their riders and perform a special set of movements.

Eggbutt T-shaped joint between the mouthpiece and rings of a bit, which stops the lips being pinched.

Ergot Hard lump that can be felt at the back of the fetlock joint.

Feather Long hair growing on the lower legs, especially in heavy breeds like the Shire or Clydesdale.

Filly Female horse under three years of age.

Flehmen Odd lip-curling gesture performed by horses and ponies when they smell or taste something unusual, or by a stallion interested in a mare.

Foal Baby horse.

Forehand Part of the horse's body in front of the saddle (see Hindquarters).

Forelock Section of the mane that falls forward between the ears and over the forehead.

Gall Sore around the belly caused by a girth that is dirty or too tight.

Gamgee Cotton wool lined with gauze, used as padding under leg bandages.

Gelding Castrated male horse.

Girth Broad strap attached to the saddle straps and placed around the horse's belly to keep the saddle in position.

Going Condition of the ground for riding on: wet ground is called soft going and very dry ground is hard going.

Green Term used to describe a young, inexperienced horse.

Gymkhana Small show with games and races for ponies and their riders.

Hackamore Western type of bridle that does not use a bit.

Halter Simple item of headgear, often made from rope, from which to lead and tie up a horse.

Hand Unit of measurement of a horse's height. One hand equals approximately 10 cm (4 in).

Headcollar Headgear made up of a noseband, headpiece and throatlatch from which to lead and tie up a horse.

Hindquarters Part of the horse's body behind the saddle (see Forehand).

Hogged mane When the mane is clipped off. Hogging is done to improve the appearance of horses with short, thick necks and coarse manes.

Keepers Small leather loops on the bridle used to hold the spare ends of the bridle straps neatly in place.

Knee rolls Pads at the front of the saddle flaps that help to keep the rider's legs in the correct position.

Laminitis Painful disease that makes the horse's feet very tender, usually caused by overeating.

Leading leg Foreleg that stretches furthest forwards in canter on a circle.

Loading Putting a horse or pony into a horsebox or trailer.

Loosebox Individual stable where a horse is kept and can be left loose.

Lunge Long rein that is attached to a special headcollar called a lungeing cavesson. The trainer sends the horse around in a circle, using a lungeing whip to move him forward.

Manège Enclosed outdoor riding arena, usually with a surface that is rideable in all weathers.

Manger Trough in a stable used for a horse's feed.

Mare Adult female horse.

Martingale Neckstrap attached between the forelegs to the girth and also the reins or noseband, to give the rider extra control.

Nappy Term used to describe a stubborn horse that will not go forward or hangs back towards his stable or other horses.

Near side Left-hand side of a horse (see Off side).

Neckstrap Strap placed around a horse's neck that a beginner can hold on to for safety. (See Breastplate, Martingale.)

New Zealand rug Tough rug for using outdoors in winter.

Novice Beginner rider or inexperienced horse.

Numnah Cotton or fleecy shaped pad used under the saddle to absorb sweat and ease pressure.

Off side Right-hand side of the horse (see Near side).

Overreaching When a hind hoof hits the heel of a front hoof, causing injury.

Pelham Type of bit used with two reins and a curb chain, which allows a stronger action than a snaffle.

Picking out Cleaning out the horse's hooves.

Points (1) Parts of the horse (see pages 32–33). (2) Extremities of a horse, such as the muzzle, tips of ears and lower legs, which are sometimes of a darker colour than the rest of the body.

Pulling a mane/tail Taking out hairs, a few at a time, to neaten the mane or tail.

Rein (1) Long strap attached to the bit and used by the rider to control the horse. (2) Direction in which horse and rider are moving around the arena, being on either the left rein or the right rein.

Roller Wide strap used around the belly to keep a rug in place.

Roman nose Convex profile, most often seen in heavy horses.

Running up the stirrups Pushing the stirrup irons up the back of the leathers and threading the leathers through the irons, to keep the stirrups tidy and safe when a horse is tacked up but not about to be ridden (see pages 62–63).

Schooling Training a horse.

Shying Sudden movement sideways after taking fright.

Sire Father of a foal.

Skipping out Speedy muck-out during the day using a skip (wicker or rubber basket) to collect the droppings.

Snaffle Largest family of bits, with one ring either side of the mouthpiece.

Sound Term used to describe a healthy horse with no breathing or lameness problems.

Stallion Uncastrated male horse.

Surcingle Narrow strap used around the belly to fasten a rug, or over the saddle for extra security when galloping or jumping.

Tack Items of saddlery used for riding.

Tacking up Putting on the tack.

Transition Change from one pace to another.

Tree Frame around which a saddle is built.

Turning out Letting a horse loose into a field.

Turnout (1) Appearance of a horse and rider, which is very important in show classes. (2) Area (usually a field) in which a horse can be let loose to graze and move around.

Vice Bad or nervous habit. Stable vices often start because a horse is bored. These include weaving, where the horse sways to and fro, and crib-biting and wind-sucking, where the horse arches his neck and sucks in air. Vices shown out riding include rearing, napping and bucking.

Wind Horse's breathing. A broken-winded horse is one with a problem in his breathing.

Wither Top of the shoulder blade, which forms a bony ridge at the base of the neck. Horses and ponies are measured from the ground to the highest point of the wither.

Yearling One-year-old horse.

INDEX

ACKNOWLEDGEMENTS

Executive Editor Trevor Davies
Executive Art Editor Leigh Jones
Editor Rachel Lawrence
Designer Anna Pow
Picture Researcher Liz Fowler
Production Controller Ian Paton
Photographer Bob Langrish